Consumer Behavior
of Individual Families
Over Two & Three Years

Studies Edited by
Richard F. Kosobud
and James N. Morgan

Monograph No. 36
Survey Research Center
Institute for Social Research
The University of Michigan

LIBRARY
University of Texas
At San Antonio

Preface

The Survey Research Center was established shortly after World War II because of the conviction that survey research through personal interviews with representative samples of the population contributes an important tool of economic research. Many of the Center's findings are based on interviews taken with a sample of respondents interviewed once. Yet, gathering information through repeated interviews with the same families represents an important additional source of findings on economic behavior. This monograph is devoted to new studies making use of the panel method.

An important impetus to this work came from an Advisory Committee established late in 1959 to guide the development of research objectives for the Center's Surveys of Consumer Finances. During the last few years the following scholars served as members of the committee for varying periods of time: Gardner Ackley, Robert Ferber, Raymond Goldsmith, Albert Hart, Walter Heller, Herbert Hyman, Lawrence Klein, Paul McCracken, Franco Modigliani, Guy Orcutt, Howard Raiffa, James Tobin, and Harold Watts. The committee was established at the time the Ford Foundation made a grant to help finance the 1960, 1961, and 1962 Surveys of Consumer Finances. It was during these surveys that the consumer panel was built up. Private financial support provided the necessary remainder of the resources to carry out the surveys. A grant from the Rockefeller Foundation for research and publication purposes facilitated the completion of these studies. It proved necessary also to call upon the reserve funds of the Survey Research Center to complete the analysis and writing. These contributions are acknowledged with gratitude.

Fellow research workers in various capacities provided assistance, comments, and criticisms which helped shape the final product. It is a pleasure to acknowledge the work of Charles F. Cannell and Morris Axelrod who directed the field staff and their interviewing, of Leslie Kish and Irene Hess who designed the sample, of Doris Muehl and Joan Scheffler who supervised the coding, and of Charles A. Lininger who supervised the three surveys of Consumer Finances. Jean King edited the manuscript to the benefit of the reader. Alice Sano spaced and typed the tables in an expert way. The responsibility for findings and interpretation rests with the authors of the various chapters.

Table of Contents

v

List of Tables and Illustrations

Tables   Page

Charts

APPENDIX A

APPENDIX B

Chapter 1

Introduction

IN THIS MONOGRAPH we present an analysis of data gathered from a panel of respondents who were interviewed in three successive Surveys of Consumer Finances. Over a thousand spending units interviewed in early 1960 were reinterviewed in early 1961 and early 1962. Data were thus made available on a number of variables that could not be measured in a single survey. These include income and saving over a two-year span, major expenditures for each of three years, buying plans and subsequent expenditures for specific commodities and changes in attitudes. The first interview (1960) thoroughly explored the respondent's income history, and the last interview (1962) included questions about short and longer range income expectations. Hence the data on change discussed here were elicited both by memory and expectation questions and by questions on reinterview.

The need for better information about the dynamics of consumer behavior in the aggregate has led to the use of micro survey data about individual consumer units. But since the macrotheories about consumer behavior are dynamic, the microdata need to be dynamic as well. A single survey can provide some data on change by asking about past changes and by asking about expectations for the future. But a respondent answering questions about himself is subject to error and bias in remembering what has happened and uncertainty in predicting what will happen. Hence, panel studies yielding repeated interviews with the same families are a better source of dynamic microdata.[1]

[1]Panel studies reported in the literature include: Marion Sobol, "Panel Mortality and Panel Bias," *Journal of the American Statistical Association,* LIV (March 1959), 52-68 (a survey Research Center study in which a panel was interviewed five times over three years); Elizabeth H. Wolgast, "Do Husbands or Wives make the purchasing Decisions," *Journal of Marketing,* XXIII (October 1958), 15, 151-58; George Katona, "Attitude Change: Instability of Response and Acquisition of Experience," *Psychological Monographs,* LXXII (1958), 1-38; Eva Mueller, "Effects of Consumer Attitudes on Purchases," *American Economic Review,* XLVII (December

1

Such panel studies have been rare because they are expensive and because the loss in response rate can produce some biases. Basic relationships generally remain relatively unbiased, however, and the data are free from some of the worst memory biases. It ought to be noted in this connection that in the studies reported in this book we have specified and estimated relationships rather than presented aggregates or averages.

The theoretical models behind the analysis presented here are general and somewhat empiristic. Some of these studies test relatively specific and structured hypotheses against the data. In others the emphasis is upon discovering which one of several theoretically relevant explanatory factors really matters, and how much. Much of the existing theoretical work on consumer behavior focuses on variables like prices and income which do not change very much even over a period as long as three years. A short-range panel cannot produce precise estimates of their effects. On the other hand, many things which change too slowly in the aggregates to be investigated can be studied in a cross section study.

Our analysis also uses more than one kind of explanatory variable, combining financial and factual data with attitudes and expectations in an attempt to explain behavior. And the panel allows us to use not just the levels of attitudes but also their changes over time. It is no longer true that only factual, financial, and demographic variables can be mea-

1957), 946-65; Eva Mueller, "Consumer Reactions to Inflation," *Quarterly Journal of Economics*, LXXIII (May 1959), 246-62; Robert Ferber, "The Role of Planning in Consumer Purchases of Durable Goods," *American Economic Review*, XLIV (December 1954), 854-74; Jean Crockett, "A New Type of Estimate of the Income Elasticity of the Demand for Food," *Proceedings of the Business and Economics Section of the American Statistical Association* (1957); and T. W. Anderson, "Probability Models for Analyzing Time Changes in Attitudes" in P. F. Lazarsfeld (ed.), *Mathematical Thinking in the Social Sciences* (Glencoe: Free Press, 1954).

The Inter-University Committee for Research on Consumer Behavior, Robert Ferber, Director, has been associated with panel studies which treat methodological and substantive aspects of saving behavior. The Federal Reserve Board of Governors has sponsored a survey of financial characteristics of consumers in 1963 that incorporated a reinterview and measured saving.

Census Current Population Studies, which cover buying plans as well as labor force data have a built in system of reinterviews. Census studies of additions and repairs have built in reinterviews largely for methodological purposes. See two articles by J. Neger and J. Waksberg, "Conditioning Effects from Repeated Household Interviews," *Journal of Marketing*, XXVIII (April 1964), 51-56; and "A Study of Response Errors in Expenditure Data from Household Surveys," *Journal of the American Statistical Association*, LIV (March 1964), 18-55.

sured and used in time series analysis and prediction. The growing archives of data that the SRC has accumulated over a long period on the attitudes and expectations of consumers can now be built into time-series analysis.[2] With considerable promise of potential payoff, the short-run dynamic relations can be built into simulation systems that use microrelations to derive macrodynamic conclusions.[3]

At the descriptive level, we can investigate individual economic histories in much greater detail with panel data than with data from one set of interviews. A research worker interested in the influence of income change upon saving and expenditures may suspect that not all income change is homogeneous in its influence. If he prepares a list of the different reasons for changes in income, the list might include the following: (a) changes in wage or salary rate, (b) changes in the number of income earners in the spending unit, (c) changes in labor force status from employment to unemployment, (d) changes in the amount of overtime worked, (e) changes in the amount of work performed or available (piece rates), and (f) changes in the amount of vacation taken. Clearly the list is not exhaustive. Simply to draw up such a list is to be made aware that there is very little information available as to the quantitative importance of these items.

Specific Studies

In Chapter 2, in a study directed by George Katona, changes in an optimism index prepared from six attitudinal questions are related to consumer expenditures and saving behavior. Measures of change in the index over one year and over two years are calculated and related to one- and two-year measures of the dependent variables. High levels of optimism are found to be directly related to consumer investment expenditures. The influence of changes in optimism requires a more subtle analysis.

The study done by James N. Morgan, described in Chapter 3, adds to our descriptive knowledge of the reasons for income change. He concludes from a study of the distributions that an appreciable amount

[2]Professor Lawrence Klein at the University of Pennsylvania has produced some encouraging results in this way.

[3]See Guy Orcutt and others, *Micro Analysis of Socio-Economic Systems* (New York: Harper and Bros., 1961).

of income change does occur from year to year, much more than one might expect from changes in unemployment. He raises the question of whether a given income change due, say, to a salary increase has an influence upon expenditures of the same quantitative significance as a given income change due, say, to more overtime work or to an extra income earner. Morgan finds by comparing the respondent's financial anticipation with experienced events, that many of the sizable fraction of spending units reporting income change from year to year anticipated these changes. The number of income surprises seem relatively few.

Some issues involved in the fulfillment of individual buying plans are discussed in Chapter 4 by Richard F. Kosobud. He examines first the accuracy of individual buying plans in predicting subsequent expenditures. Buying plans expressed in 1961 tended to overestimate the amount of expenditures over the next twelve months. It will be important to learn whether this overestimation persists in other years, for if it does it is a type of predictive error that could be taken into account by forecasters. In the main part of this chapter Kosobud describes how the difference between planned and reported expenditures is related to unanticipated movements in income and prices. Fulfillment relationships are estimated in an attack on these problems. A noteworthy feature of this research is the attempt to measure directly unanticipated movements in prices and in income from changes in the respondent's anticipations of these events.

In Chapter 5 a measure of consumer saving is obtained by smoothing out annual data. Two-year saving and income measures are prepared by Kosobud and John B. Lansing. They conclude that estimates of two-year saving relationship tend to be consistent with estimates based upon one-year measures, a finding which is of special interest because it has been alleged in the past that one-year measures of these variables contain large errors of measurement. The principal contribution of this study is a systematic exploration of the influence of liquid assets upon the saving rate. This influence appears to affect low income units and high income units in opposite ways. Among low income units the presence of liquid assets appears to depress the saving rate; among high income units they appear, if anything, to increase the rate. This result has been observed before. Kosobud and Lansing investigate a number of biases which could rob this finding of any behavioral significance. They conclude that, even after allowance is made for distorting factors, these saving relationships persist.

In the last chapter Morgan draws together a number of explanatory variables that have been described in the monograph. Evaluating the relative contribution of each variable to a reduction of the contingency surrounding consumer expenditures and saving, he arrives at a number of detailed conclusions. His study indicates the importance of disaggregating the total sample into more homogeneous groups. Morgan finds that the group of homeowners with large assets tend to save at a high rate, other things equal.

Appendices

Several methodological aspects of panel surveys are discussed in Appendix A, aspects which bear upon possible errors of measurement and panel bias. To assist the reader, a brief account of the data-processing steps are presented and relevant portions of the questionnaires are reproduced.

Frequency distributions of selected characteristics of the panel are presented by Albert M. Marckwardt in Appendix B. He compares these characteristics to those of spending units that moved away and were not interviewed and to some known characteristics of spending units that refused to be interviewed. He finds that the panel tended to contain more older people, more homeowners, and more high income people than the population as a whole. These findings were expected in view of the reinterview design and the fact that movers were not followed nor were younger units introduced into the sample. The distributions presented in Appendix B indicate that there is considerable variation in the range of values of the major variables in our models, a variation which is important in our search for behavioral relationships.

Chapter 2
The Influence of Attitudes on the Purchasing Behavior of Individudal Consumers*

IT HAS BECOME well established that buying plans and consumer attitudes are useful in predicting the trend of aggregate purchases of durable goods. The effects of consumer attitudes and expectations on the purchases of the individual consumer are also of great interest. Using data from the 1960-62 panel study we shall describe in this chapter the influence on purchases of durable goods by individuals of (1) their inflationary expectations and (2) changes in their attitudes.

Inflationary Expectations

In order to determine expectations about prices, each member of the panel was asked two questions in January 1960:

1. Whether (in his opinion) the prices of things he buys will go up or down during the next year, and
2. Whether they will go up or down during the next five years.

Each member was asked these questions again in January 1962. The most inflation-minded respondents were those who replied all four times that "prices will go up" and the least inflation-minded were those who never gave this answer. These two groups of respondents (and an intermediate group as well) are compared in Table 2-1 with regard to their expenditures on durable goods in 1960 and 1961.

*Prepared by the Survey Research Center staff under the supervision of George Katona.

6

The dependent variable in Table 2-1 is the proportion of income spent on durables. An income effect is not eliminated, although the higher the income the more common are inflationary expectations and the larger the proportion of income spent on durables. Income is therefore used as a control variable. (Respondents with low incomes occasionally spend a very high percentage of their income on durables; data on respondents with a two year income of less than $5000 are not included in Table 2-1.)

In the middle income group (two-year income of $5000-7499) there appear to be no significant differences in expenditures on durables between those with inflationary expectations and those who do not expect inflation. In the higher income group, however, people with inflationary attitudes appear to spend smaller proportions of their incomes on durables than those who do not expect inflation[1]. For many people, expectations of unchanged prices are associated with an optimistic outlook and extensive purchases; inflation, on the other hand, is associated with uncertainty, pessimism, and the postponement of some purchases.

Changes in Consumer Attitudes

Three studies of the effects of change in individual consumer attitudes were carried out using the 1960-62 panel data. They are:

1. The relationship of 1960 expenditures on durables to change in attitudes from early 1960 to early 1961.
2. The relationship of 1961 expenditures on durables to change in attitudes from early 1960 to early 1961.
3. The relationship of expenditures on durables over a two-year period to attitude change over the same period (early 1960 to early 1962).

These three studies will be discussed below.

In order to determine individual change in attitudes, an "optimism index" was constructed for each respondent on the basis of responses given in early 1960, 1961, and 1962. The six questions which make up

[1] This finding is in line with earlier work by Eva Mueller, "Consumer Reactions to Inflation," *Quarterly Journal of Economics*, **LXXII** (May, 1959), 246-62; and in line with theoretical considerations by George Katona in *The Powerful Consumer* (New York: McGraw-Hill Book Company, 1960), Chapter 12.

the Survey Research Center's Index of Consumer Attitudes were used to rank each respondent.[2] Optimistic answers were scored 2, middle-level answers were scored 1, and pessimistic answers were scored 0. Thus the range of scores was 0 to 12. Table 2-2, part a. shows the frequency distribution of respondents in the three groups that were formed on the basis of this index: (1) those whose attitudes were optimistic, (2) those whose attitudes were "medium," (3) and those who were pessimistic.

In order to describe change in respondents' optimism, two variables were derived from the optimism index: (1) change in optimism over a one-year period (1960) and (2) change in optimism over a two-year period (1960-1961). The frequency distribution of respondents with various kinds of attitude change are shown in Table 2-2, parts b and c.

Change in Attitudes over 1960 Related to
Expenditures in Same Year

In Table 2-3 we show the results of the first study of the relationship of changes in attitudes to expenditures on durables. The 1960

---

[2] **Portions** of the questionnaire containing these questions are reproduced in Appendix A. The six questions utilized in the index were:

(a) We are interested in how people are getting along financially these days. Would you say that you and your family are better off or worse off financially than you were *a year ago?*

(b) Now looking ahead, do you think that *a year from now* you people will be better off financially, or worse off, or just about the same as now?

(c) Now turning to business conditions in the country as a whole—do you think that during the next twelve months we'll have good times financially or bad times, or what?

(d) Looking ahead, which would you say is more likely—that in the country as a whole we will have continuous good times during the next five years or so—or that we will have periods of widespread unemployment or depression, or what?

(e) About the things people buy for their house—I mean furniture, house furnishings, refrigerator, stove, TV, and things like that. In general, do you think now is a good or bad time to buy such large household items? and

(f) Now speaking of prices in general, I mean the prices of the things you buy—do you think they will go up in the next year or go down, or stay where they are now?

The procedures for preparation of the index are explained in George Katona and Eva Mueller, *Consumer Expectations 1953-1956* (Ann Arbor: Survey Research Center, 1956).

expenditures of seven groups of respondents are differentiated by changes in their attitudes from early 1960 to early 1961. On the basis of median expenditures, or the figuring of zero or low expenditures, the constant optimists (OO) appear to have spent more than the middlings (MM), who in turn spent more than the pessimists (PP). Attitudes at the beginning of the year appear to have been more influential than the attitudes at the end of the year: OO are larger spenders than MO, MM larger than PM, OM larger than MM, and OP much larger than PP. In fact, the groups OP and MP seem to be uninfluenced by their final attitudes (which may have developed early in 1961 with the oncoming recession).

Table 2-4 reproduces the data in Table 2-3 with income differences eliminated. (Because of the small number of cases studied, Table 2-4 shows three attitudinal groupings instead of seven.) For the group with incomes of $7500 or more the data conform to expectations; in the $4000-7499 income group practically no differences are found.

Change in Attitudes over 1960 Related to
Expenditures in Succeeding Year

This study investigates the forecasting value of two attitude measurements when the dependent variable is the rate of expenditures on durables in the period following that bracketed by the attitude measurements. Table 2-5 shows the 1961 durables expenditure of seven groups of respondents, differentiated by changes in their attitudes from early 1960 to early 1961.

Groups OO and OM have the highest median expenditures, group OO by far the lowest zero expenditures, and MO the highest large expenditures. Groups PP and PM show the smallest expenditures, Again, group OP does not seem to fit; the expenditures of this group indicate that there is value in looking at two preceding attitude measures.

The data by income groups present a good fit (Table 2-6). The median declines, and the frequency of nonspenders increases progressively if one proceeds from optimistic to pessimistic groups.

Change in Attitudes over 1960 and 1961
Related to Expenditures during Those Two Years

Respondents characterized as "Optimism high" appear to have been more frequent spenders than the group labeled "Optimism medium," who in turn exceed the "Optimism low" group. Yet the groups with rising or falling optimism do not seem to have behaved according to expectations (Table 2-7, top half).

The findings are similar when only upper income people, rather than all respondents are studied (Table 2-7, bottom half).

Summary

It appears that individuals' expenditures on durable goods, expressed in percentages of their incomes, are influenced by their attitudes, as measured by level and change in the Survey Research Center's Index of Consumer Attitudes. Yet the correspondence between optimists and large spenders, or between pessimists and small spenders, is not complete in every instance.

This incomplete correspondence is probably the result of certain factors not eliminated in these studies (e.g., many purhcases of durables are not discretionary, but are compelled by circumstances). It may also result from the fact that the measures of attitudes are crude.

Table 2-1

PROPORTION OF TWO-YEAR INCOME SPENT ON DURABLES,
BY INCOME AND INFLATIONARY EXPECTATIONS
(Percentage distribution)

Ratio of durables expenditures to income during 1960-61 (in per cent)	Inflationary expectations		
	Exclusive[a]	Predominant[b]	None[c]
	Two-year average income $5000-7499		
Under 4	17	17	12
4-9	11	21	20
10-19	23	25	26
20-29	14	10	15
30 or more	35	27	27
Total	100	100	100
Number of cases	61	97	53
	Two-year average income $7500-15,000		
Under 4	31	13	22
4-9	21	14	18
10-19	22	33	14
20-29	10	17	14
30 or more	16	23	32
Total	100	100	100
Number of cases	101	126	57

[a]When asked in January 1960 (and again in January 1962) whether they expected prices to go up, stay the same or go down in the "next year" and in the "next five years" these respondents answered "up" four times.

[b]Answered "up" two or three times; never answered "down."

[c]Never answered "up."

Table 2-2

DISTRIBUTION OF RESPONDENTS ON THE OPTIMISM INDEX

	Early 1960	Early 1961	Early 1962
a. Optimism index for each year			
Optimistic (scoring 10-12)	21	15	22
Medium (scoring 7-9)	51	48	49
Pessimistic (scoring 0-6)	28	37	29
Total	100	100	100
Number of cases	1059	1059	1059

b. Change in optimism from 1960 to 1961

OO[a]	Optimistic in 1960 and 1961	6
MO	Medium in 1960 and optimistic in 1961	9
PO	Pessimistic in 1960 and optimistic in 1961	
MM	Medium in 1960 and 1961	26
OM	Optimistic in 1960 and medium in 1961	11
PM	Pessimistic in 1960 and medium in 1961	11
PP	Pessimistic in 1960 and 1961	15
OP	Optimistic in 1960 and pessimistic in 1961	
MP	Medium in 1960 and pessimistic in 1961	22
	Total	100

[a]The first letter refers to 1960 and the second letter to 1961.

c. Change in optimism over 3 years (early 1960 to early 1962)

Optimism high (OOO, OOM, OMO, MOO)[a]	13
Optimism medium (MMM, MPM, MOM)	26
Optimism low (PPP, PPM, PMP, MPP)	27
Optimism rising (PMO, POO, MMO, PPO, PMM, POM, MPO)	17
Optimism falling (MOP, OMM, MMP, OOP, OPP, OMP, OPM)	16
Other (POP, OPO)	1
Total	100

[a]The first letter refers to 1960, the second letter to 1961, and the third letter to 1962.

Table 2-3

PROPORTION OF 1960 INCOME SPENT ON DURABLES,
BY ATTITUDE CHANGE OVER SAME YEAR

(Percentage distribution of 1059 panel members)

Ratio of durables expenditure to income during 1960 (in per cent)	All	Constant optimism OO	Increased to optimism MO, PO	middle-range optimism MM	Decreased to middle range optimism OM	Increased to middle range optimism PM	Constant pessimism PP	Decreased to pessimism OP, MP
				Attitude change of panel member, early 1960 to early 1961				
Zero	33	24	32	31	28	37	46	32
1-9	30	34	26	32	34	28	27	31
10-29	24	27	30	27	29	24	16	20
30 or more	12	15	11	9	9	11	11	16
N.A.	1	*	1	1	*	*	*	1
Total	100	100	100	100	100	100	100	100
Median (in per cent)	4.5	7.5	6.0	4.3	5.8	3.8	1.8	4.5
Number of cases	1059	65	93	277	111	116	161	236

*Less than one-half of one per cent.

Table 2-4

PROPORTION OF 1960 INCOME SPENT ON DURABLES
BY ATTITUDE CHANGE OVER SAME YEAR AND INCOME GROUP
(Percentage distribution of 1059 panel members)

Ratio of durables expenditures to income during 1960	Attitude change of panel members, early 1960 to early 1961[a]					
	1960 income $4000-7499			1960 income $7500 or more		
	OO, MO, PO, OM	MM	PM, PP, OP, MP	OO, MO, PO, OM	MM	PM, PP, OP, MP
Zero	30	34	30	12	19	23
1-9	35	34	33	39	34	40
10-29	22	22	22	38	35	28
30 or more	12	10	15	11	10	9
N.A.	1	*	*	*	2	*
Total	100	100	100	100	100	100
Median (in per cent)	4.1	3.2	5.5	9.3	7.9	5.9
Number of cases	103	103	181	112	105	119

*Less than one-half of one per cent.
[a]O = optimistic; M = middle range of optimism; P = pessimistic. First letter represents attitude in early 1960; second letter represents attitude in early 1961.

Table 2-5

PROPORTION OF 1961 INCOME SPENT ON DURABLES
BY ATTITUDE CHANGE DURING PREVIOUS YEAR

(Percentage distribution of 1059 panel members)

Ratio of durables expenditure to income during 1961 (in per cent)	Attitude change of panel members, early 1960 to early 1961[a]							
	All	OO	MO, PO	MM	OM	PM	PP	OP, MP
Zero	39	20	32	35	30	50	47	43
1-9	34	51	35	39	36	30	28	28
10-29	16	21	15	17	23	9	13	17
30 or more	10	8	18	8	10	11	10	10
N.A.	1	*	*	1	1	*	2	2
Total	100	100	100	100	100	100	100	100
Median (in per cent)	2.8	4.9	3.5	3.0	4.9	0.5	1.4	3.1
Number of cases	1059	66	93	276	111	116	161	236

*Less than one-half of one per cent.

[a] O = optimistic; M = middle range of optimism; P = pessimistic.
First letter represents attitude in early 1960; second letter,
early 1961.

Table 2-6

PROPORTION OF 1961 INCOME SPENT ON DURABLES,
BY ATTITUDE CHANGE OVER PRIOR YEAR AND INCOME GROUP
(Percentage distribution of 1059 panel members)

Ratio of durables expenditures to income during 1961	Attitude change of panel members early 1960 to early 1961[a]					
	1960-1961 average income of $4000-7499			1960-1961 average income of $7500 or over		
	OO, MO, PO, OM	MM	PM, PP, OP, MP	OO, MO, PO, OM	MM	PM, PP, OP, MP
Zero	22	32	41	17	22	28
1-9	45	31	33	44	51	41
10-29	16	20	14	29	23	17
30 or more	17	16	10	9	4	13
N.A.	*	1	2	1	*	1
Total	100	100	100	100	100	100
Median	5.2	3.9	2.8	6.1	4.4	3.3
Number of cases	102	102	183	110	104	114

*Less than one-half of one per cent.

[a]O = optimistic; M = middle range of optimism; P = pessimistic. First letter represents attitudes in early 1960, and the second represents attitudes in early 1961.

Table 2-7

PROPORTION OF TWO-YEAR INCOME SPENT ON DURABLES,
BY CHANGE IN ATTITUDE OVER SAME PERIOD

(Percentage distribution)

Ratio of durables expenditures to income during 1960-1961 (in per cent)	All cases	Level of optimism over 1960 and 1961				
		High	Medium	Low	Rising	Falling
		All panel members				
Zero	22	11	21	29	21	19
1-9	41	45	42	37	41	42
10-29	29	30	32	23	32	31
30 or more	7	14	4	9	5	6
Not ascertained	1	*	1	2	1	2
Total	100	100	100	100	100	100
Median (in per cent)	6.5	7.9	6.3	5.0	6.7	6.6
Number of cases	1059	134	277	283	183	173
		Panel members whose two-year income averaged $7500 or more				
Zero		4	5	12	12	12
1-9		46	55	45	46	48
10-29		40	36	37	39	34
30 or more		10	2	4	3	4
Not ascertained		*	2	2	*	2
Total		100	100	100	100	100
Median (in per cent)		9.5	7.7	7.8	7.8	7.0
Number of cases		68	81	51	69	59

*Less than one-half of one per cent.

Chapter 3

The Anatomy of Income Change*

A GREAT DEAL of attention has been paid recently to the problem of measuring ability to pay and to possible biases resulting from the use of one-year's income as a measure of economic status. The purpose of this chapter is to show some of the rich variety of kinds of income change, to develop some classifications of types of income change, and to describe the frequency and impact of income fluctuations in subgroups of the population. Some tentative findings about the effects of different kinds of income change on spending and saving behavior are discussed here. (A much more complete analysis of these effects appears in Chapter 6 where they have a chance to prove their importance in competition with attitudinal, demographic, and other economic variables.)

We shall make use in this chapter of one of the advantages of repeated interviews with spending units. It is a simple but important one: a respondent can be asked many more questions during three interviews separated each by a year than during one without risking loss of his good will or accuracy of recall. Three kinds of questions about income change were asked of respondents in the panel:

1. Questions dealing with long-run, lifetime patterns of experienced income change.
2. Questions dealing with a middle-range or ten-year pattern of income change as experienced and as anticipated.
3. Questions dealing with shorter-run or year-to-year income as experienced and as anticipated.

A number of questions can be raised with respect to the three kinds of data on income change: questions involving the reliability of such data in some general sense, the descriptive value of such data, and the use-

---

*This study was designed and the chapter written by James N. Morgan.

18

fulness of such data as measures of variables entering into consumer behavior. The first two kinds of questions are considered in this chapter.

Income Change From Memory Questions

A single cross-section survey can be used for relatively dynamic analysis by using memory questions on past changes, at least for some things. In order to explain future purchase plans and current attitudes, one can ask the respondent whether he is better or worse off than a year earlier, or whether he is making more or less money now than he was a year earlier. In order to explain expenditures or saving during a period prior to the interview, however, we need to know whether the previous year's income was larger or smaller than the income for the year before that. Sometimes dollar income reports are asked for both years and income changes estimated from these reports. Sometimes (and always for those who cannot remember a dollar income year before last) we ask whether the income was larger or smaller than the previous year and whether the change was large or small.

Experience has shown that the broader such questions are, the more likely the "no change" response. Indeed, validity studies have shown a tendency for people to remember the past as more like the present than it really was. Memory questions about short-run changes will elicit "no change" responses from one-fourth to one-third of the respondents, whereas computations based on two interviews with the same people show only one-sixth or one-seventh with income changes of less than 5 per cent. In addition, for a substantial number of respondents (more than a tenth) a comparison of the two interviews reveals disagreement even about the direction of the change.

This does not mean that memory questions are the only source of trouble. In separate interviews there are two chances for error or failure to report some component of income. Nevertheless, it seems likely that misunderstandings about which year is being compared with which (Does larger mean an increase or a decrease in income?) and problems of remembering make the memory reports less reliable than the results of separate interviews.

Such measures are not useless, of course. The group that reported higher income (one-half of the panel) and the group that reported lower income (one-sixth of the panel) can be compared with those who reported no change, or with each other. In addition, people's perceptions or feelings about the direction in which their incomes have changed is of some relevance.

Longer Term Income History

If one year's income may sometimes be an inaccurate reflection of a man's financial status, prospects, and history, then it may pay to find out about his distant past income and longer-term future expectations. In the middle interview taken in early 1961, questions were asked about income in 1960, 1955, 1947, 1940, 1928 and 1920. Not everyone was in the labor force in the earlier years: only 14 per cent reported receiving an income in 1920 and only 23 per cent in 1928. The sample size for the 1961 survey was 1981 spending units including 1059 panel members. In the sections on long-run income changes we shall make use of this larger sample. Some data from these questions, showing the patterns of income change reported by people for earlier years and for certain age spans, were given in *1961 Survey of Consumer Finances* (Ann Arbor, Michigan: Survey Research Center, 1962).

By heroic estimation of decile points and interpolation to estimate incomes at given ages, it is possible to produce data for each individual over 40 on change in decile position from age 30 to age 40. However, this change needs to be looked at separately for each generation (cohort), since it depends on the historical period when the respondent was reaching middle age. Table 3-1 shows that those who were developing their careers before the Depression (last column) moved up the salary ladder if they had any education beyond grade school. Those who were hit by the Depression in their formative years had small improvements unrelated to their education (third column). But those who have grown up in more recent years have moved *up* the relative income scale if they were well educated and *down* if they were uneducated.

It has often been pointed out that the variation of income among individuals of different ages in a cross section does not reflect the experience over time of any individual because two offsetting things happen:

1. Older people are more subject to unemployment, illness, and so forth.
2. As time passes, the level of wages, particularly money wages, rises, and for the average man this may more than offset the effects of chronological age.

Table 3-1

Change in Income Decile Position of Median Spending Unit Head
Between the Ages of 30 and 40, By Educational Attainment

Educational attainment of head	Age of SU head in early 1961			
	40-44	45-54	55-64	65 or older
Eight years of schooling or less	- .9	+.1	+.3	+ .4
Some high school	-1.0	-.3	+.3	+1.0
High school graduate	- .1	-.5	+.3	+1.0
Some college	+ .3	*	+.3	+1.5
College degree	+ .3	+.3	+.2	+1.0
Per cent of all cases	20	36	25	19

*Less than one-tenth of a decile interval.

These forces are illustrated in Table 3-2. Reading across the table, one finds the patterns of incomes reported for the same year for people of different ages. Clearly, median income drops after age 45. Reading down the table, one finds that for any one generation (cohort), there is generally a continuous increase in earnings up to the present except for people in the two older cohorts. This indicates that for people over 54 the age effect has exceeded the general increase. The implication is that while there may be something to the notion of long-term general increase in income, it is more than offset, in recent American experience, by the depressing effects of advanced age of earnings.

There would appear to be little point (and as a matter of fact, few methods are available) to check the validity of these long-run reported income experiences. One indirect test of the data are the results they

CONSUMER BEHAVIOR

Table 3-2

MEDIAN INCOME IN SELECTED YEARS BY COHORT GROUPS

Median income[a] Year	All cases	Age of spending unit head in early 1961					
		18-24	25-34	35-44	45-54	55-64	65 or older
1928						$1350	$1560
1940					$1920	2090	1770
1947	$2110			$2890	3720	3200	2870
1955	3800		$3510	4540	4920	4060	1950
1960	4590	$3310	5150	5870	5300	3910	1800
Number of cases	1981	169	407	451	393	290	271

[a]Interpolated, except when in the lowest bracket which includes zeros.

are capable of yielding, and the patterns revealed in Tables 3-1 and 3-2 seem sensible.

Middle-range Income Experience and Expectations

Further inquiry was made in the 1961 survey as to middle-range income history and expectations: The question asked was:

"Has your income been quite steady during the last ten years or so, or has it been going up, or down, or changing from time to time?"

(For those working less than 10 years the question was: "Since you began working full time, has your income been going up, or down, or changing from time to time?")

And earlier in the interview the question asked was:

"During the next ten years or so, do you think your earnings will rise gradually, go up and down from year to year or fall or what?"

Of the spending units in the panel, two-tenths were headed by re-tired people or housewives who were not asked these questions; in addition, the heads of nearly one-tenth of the units in the panel were unable to say what they expected to happen to their incomes (Table 3-3). Fifty per cent of the panel expected their incomes to go up, and only ten per cent expected their incomes to decline or even fluctuate. Another ten per cent (approximately) expected no change.

Looking to the past, half of the panel reported increases in income, 15 per cent reported no change, and a third reported declines (steady or irregular) or fluctuating incomes. Examination of the distribution of ten-year anticipations within income experience in the past ten years reveals that respondents who reported prior upward income trends were more likely to report anticipations of upward trends in the future than others in the sample. However, for each group reporting prior income experience, the proportion expecting future income increases exceeds any other anticipation. For groups reporting anticipations and past in-come experiences (excluding those for whom answers were inappro-priate or not available) it is observable that panel members anticipated

Table 3-3

EXPECTATIONS ABOUT EARNINGS FOR THE NEXT TEN YEARS CONDITIONALLY DISTRIBUTED
WITHIN REPORTED INCOME EXPERIENCE OVER THE PAST TEN YEARS

(Percentage distribution of spending units interviewed early in 1961)

Expectations about earnings in next 10 years	All SU's in panel	General trend of income reported for past 10 years				
		Income up	Income steady	Income down	Income fluctuated	Not available or inappropriate
Will rise	50	68	31	22	42	12
Will stay about the same	11	10	20	7	12	4
Will fall	6	5	7	8	6	*
Will fluctuate	5	4	3	4	12	*
Not available or head is retired or a housewife	28	13	39	60	28	84
Total	100	100	100	100	100	100
Per cent of 1059 panel members	100	50	15	9	19	7

*Zero or less than one half of one per cent.

future increases in income more frequently than they reported upward trends in the past.

In asking respondents about their expected income during the next ten years, we are asking a question to which not all respondents have given much thought. And if they have definite opinions, these may not be the kind of income expectations which enter into spending and saving decisions. Some of the limitations of the long-run income expectation variable may be discussed in terms of Table 3-4 in which expectations are distributed within age. The data are obtained from surveys conducted in 1963 and enable us to draw conclusions based upon a larger sample of 3234 families. The proportion who say they don't know or can't say about their income anticipations increases with age and makes up about 6 per cent of the total sample. These people taken together with those who say their expectations depend upon other considerations (''depends'') make up about 10 per cent of the sample. It does seem prudent, therefore, to view these long-run anticipations as very likely differing in a qualitative sense from short-run anticipations. We do have evidence that the group anticipating increases in income over the next ten years exhibited saving behavior different from others: their marginal propensity to save was higher than others and the possession of liquid assets appeared to shift their savings schedules even higher.[1]

A note of caution is in order about these interpretations of these income changes. A reinterview panel has certain biases which underestimate the amount of change. Our panel comprises a sample of about 1000 people who did not move between January 1960 and March 1962, and we know that people who do not move are somewhat older and have more stable incomes.

Types of Short Run Income

''(First) the classification of income into permanent and transitory components is a rather primitive one. Surely the response of consumption to changes in income due to retirement, to unemployment, to windfalls from gifts or capital gains, and

---

[1]The interested reader may turn to Table 5-4, Chapter 5 and the related discussion.

Table 3-4

EARNING TREND DURING NEXT 10 YEARS

(Percentage distribution of spending units)

Earning trend during next 10 years[a]	All families	Age of head in 1963				
		18-24	25-34	35-44	Under 45	45 or older
Rise gradually; rise	43	86	74	60	69	22
Stay the same or go up	2	1	2	2	2	2
Stay the same, about the same	14	2	7	12	8	18
Stay the same or go down	2	*	1	1	1	2
Fall gradually, fall	9	1	1	3	2	15
Depends	3	1	3	4	3	3
Go up and down from year to year; fluctuate	4	3	5	6	5	3
Don't know, can't say	6	2	4	7	6	7
Not ascertained	2	2	2	2	2	2
Head is retired or a housewife	15	2	1	3	2	26
Total	100	100	100	100	100	100
Number of cases	3234	207	564	689	1460	1768
Share of each age group in the number who expect income to rise during next 10 years	100	13	29	30	72	28

*Less than one-half of one per cent.

[a]Data are the average frequencies of replies obtained from the January-February 1963 and August 1963 surveys. The question was "During the next ten years or so do you think (HEAD'S) earnings will rise, go up and down from year to year, or fall, or what?"

to changes in labor force participation of secondary workers in the family, cannot all be the same. Our knowledge of the effects of employment changes or changes in age distribution on saving would surely be enhanced if we sought data which differentiated these two causes of transitory variations in income."[2]

Turning now to this panel of 1059 spending units which reported income for the years 1959-1961, Table 3-5 shows the actual number of units who reported each of various kinds of change. (Move the decimal point one place to the left in order to convert number of cases to approximate percentages). There is a large amount of change, not only affecting the head, but also of the hours and earnings of the wife and of others in the unit. Some of the changes are changes to another income group (bracket), which has the disadvantage of excluding some substantial changes within brackets and including some small changes across the bracket boundaries. Nevertheless, bracket data probably underestimate the total amount of change.

The brackets used in the variable "weeks worked" were 50 to 52 weeks, 48 to 49 weeks, 40 to 47 weeks, 27 to 39 weeks, 14 to 26 weeks, and 13 weeks or less.

Very few spending unit heads worked less than 40 weeks in any one of the three years, so that any changes in weeks worked we missed because they remained within a bracket, were largely small changes. Only movements of less than 5 per cent are possible within the brackets covering 50 to 52 weeks, or 48 to 49 weeks. Hence most major changes in employment would move the individual to a different bracket on "weeks worked," and indeed most of them would involve movements to or from one of the top brackets (full employment).

The vast bulk of those reporting no change in weeks of work were of course those who worked full time both years of the pair.

The most interesting question raised by Table 3-5 is the connection between changed weeks of work and changed earnings. A simple interpretation is that a change in earnings without an associated change in weeks worked means a change in rate of pay, and that this may be more likely to be permanent than changed amounts of work. But why should reports of lower earnings be so much more frequent than reports of

[2]J. S. Duesenberry, "Comments" in *Conference on Consumption and Saving* (Philadelphia: University of Pennsylvania Press, 1960), Vol. II, p. 189.

Table 3-5

NUMBER OF SPENDING UNITS REPORTING VARIOUS CHANGES
IN INCOME AND EMPLOYMENT

(Panel of 1059 spending units, 1960-1962)

Income characteristic	1959 to 1960[a]		1960 to 1961[a]	
	Higher in 1960	Lower in 1960	Higher in 1961	Lower in 1961
Total spending unit income[b]	473	340	507	307
Spending unit in different income group[c]	293	229	292	194
Earnings of spending unit head[b]	404	323	388	417
Wife's income in different group[c]	123	96	119	105
Employment experience of SU head				
Weeks worked full time to a different group[d]	118	111	95	103
Weeks worked full or part time to a different group[d]	109	108	91	85

[a]Cases for which relevant information was not obtained are not included.

[b]Excludes changes of 5 per cent or less.

[c]The income groups are: under $1000; 1000-1999; 2000-2999; 3000-3999; 4000-4999; 5000-5999; 6000-7499; 7500-9999; 10,000-14,999; 15,000 and over.

[d]The work-week groups are 13 weeks or less, 14-26, 27-39, 40-47, 48-49, and 50-52 weeks.

fewer weeks worked? A plausible interpretation is that second jobs, overtime, and piece rates allow a drop in earnings without reducing reported weeks of work below 50. A substantial number of people (more than a third) report working more than 2000 hours a year (50 forty-hour weeks).[3]

Table 3-6 shows the change in weeks worked for spending unit heads grouped according to patterns of change in earned income. The most startling thing is the large fraction of cases where there is a change in earnings of more than 5 per cent either up or down without any corresponding shift in weeks of work. Hence unemployment explains very little of the changes in earnings.

The detailed data show that the number of movements away from or back to "full employment" is quite small. Additional light on the restricted meaning of 50 weeks or more work as a definition of full employment is given by what happens when one asks people whether they would like more work. Such an open question was asked in the 1963 Survey of Consumer Finances, and substantial proportions of that national cross section indicated a desire for more work.[4] The proportion was only 5 per cent for college graduates, however, indicating that the much larger proportions among the less educated were not just stereotyped answers.

When interrelated events such as changes in the hours and earnings of head, wife, and others occur, one can look at all their patterns. But if a single set of categories is desired, then some assignment of priorities is essential. We decided that changes in the earnings of the head and in the number of weeks he worked were most important, since he is the major earner and since changes in his earnings are less likely to reflect family changes such as grown sons leaving home, wife having a baby, or the wife deciding to work half time while children are in school.

Furthermore, even though many changes in earnings of the head were reported without a reported change in weeks of work, we decided to study separately the cases where there was a combination of change in earnings and change in weeks of work. There may still be several

[3]See James N. Morgan, Martin H. David, Wilbur J. Cohen, and Harvey E. Brazer, *Income and Welfare in the United States* (New York: McGraw-Hill Book Company, Inc., 1962), p. 83.

[4]See 1963 *Survey of Consumer Finances* (Ann Arbor, Michigan: Survey Research Center, 1964).

Table 3-6

NUMBER IN PANEL REPORTING CHANGE IN WEEKS HEAD WORKED
BY CHANGE IN HEAD'S EARNED INCOME
(Panel of 1059 spending units, 1960-1962)

Change in weeks head worked full or part time, 1959 to 1960	Change in head's earned income from 1959 to 1960		
	At least 5 per cent more	Same[a]	At least 5 per cent less
To a higher bracket	82	10	15
In same bracket	279	171	193
To a lower bracket	23	19	66

Change in weeks head worked full or part time, 1960 to 1961	Change in head's earned income from 1960 to 1961		
	At least 5 per cent more	Same[a]	At least 5 per cent less
To a higher bracket	50	17	15
In same bracket	299	180	167
To a lower bracket	21	11	50

[a]Change in number of weeks worked full time or part time was less than 5 per cent.

different reasons for change in earnings only (change in rate of pay or change in overtime, extra job, return from self-employment, etc.), but it seems likely that the reason for a combination of changes in both work and earnings would be a change in employment to less than full employment or back toward it again.

Table 3-7 gives a distribution of the panel according to such a priority sequence. The groups are mutually exclusive, and hence the number of cases is understated in which the wife earned more or less (Groups 5 and 6) because some of these cases are included in the category in which the husband's income changed. And the small number of cases in Groups 7 and 8 where spending unit income went up or down by 5 per cent or more reflect the exclusion of all cases where the head's earnings changed by 5 per cent or more, or the wife's income moved to a different bracket. The number of cases left where none of the prior things happen (123 or 131) is somewhat smaller than the number where spending unit income changes by less than 5 per cent, because some of the individual income changes may have offset each other within the unit. For instance, Marion Sobol found that wives sometimes go to work when their husbands run into difficulty finding work.[5]

To what extent are the data in Table 3-7 reliable? The use of a re-interview panel avoids the necessity for asking a man his income for the year before last, but since the income detail is asked for each of two years on two different occasions, the number of possible errors is somewhat larger. An error in a difference can arise from an error in either of the two reports. There are eight possible combinations of errors in terms of direction for the two reports, six of which would cause two incomes that are equal to appear different. The other two combinations might also have the same effect if the errors were of different sizes.

If the incomes were actually different, errors are equally likely to increase or decrease the estimated change. Hence the data presented may well exaggerate the instability of income to the extent that different errors in reporting in the two years create errors in estimates of change. Similar considerations apply to weeks of work.

[5]Marion Sobol, "Correlates of Present and Expected Future Work Status of Married Women" (unpublished Ph.D. dissertation, Dept. of Economics, University of Michigan), 1960.

Table 3-7

A PRIORITY CLASSIFICATION OF INCOME CHANGE
ACCORDING TO INFERRED MAJOR REASON

(Panel of 1059 spending units, 1960-1962)

Kinds of income change[a]	1959 to 1960	1960 to 1961
Head's earnings higher		
1. No increase in full or part time weeks worked	312	321
2. Increase in full or part time weeks worked	92	67
Head's earnings lower		
3. No fewer full or part time weeks worked	320	335
4. Fewer full or part time weeks worked	103	82
Head's earnings same		
5. Wife earned more (whether from starting work, working more, or earning more per hour)	23	23
6. Wife earned less (whether from leaving labor force, working less, or earning less per hour)	20	17
Earnings of head and wife the same		
7. Other sources increased unit's income	23	32
8. Other sources decreased unit's income	13	10
None of the above:		
9. Unit income changed less than 5 per cent	123	131
10. Relevant data not ascertained	30	41
Total	1059	1059

[a]Income change calculations were carried out as follows: for the
spending unit head the ratio of reported dollar amounts was computed. For the wife when present an income change was recorded as
a movement out of one income bracket into another. The income
brackets were: under $500; 500-999; 1000-1999; 2000-2999; 3000-
4999; 5000-7499; 7500-9999; 10,000 and over.

There may also be some errors in editing unusual cases, for example, where income is considered earned income one year, but transfer income the other. However, an investigation of some cases of change in income without change in weeks worked revealed mostly cases of "less extra work," "more overtime," piece work (e.g., car washer), or self-employment.

It is doubtful that errors in reporting account for any substantial part of the reported changes. We have seen earlier that even on the basis of superficial memory questions only 30 per cent say their income for last year was the same as the year before, and inquiring about dollar incomes for the two years cuts that proportion in half. It is likely that people forget smaller changes which actually occur, particularly if they are changes in the income of the wife or some other source.

What stands out, then, is a very frequent impact of change in income from one year to the next, and most of it is *not* associated with movements into and out of unemployment as usually defined. In addition to the changes in income not associated with unemployment or with recovery from unemployment, there remain a substantial number of changes to and from unemployment situations, and an appreciable number of other changes even in spending units where the husband's income did not change.

Who Has What Kind of Income Change?

If our categories of types of income change can be accepted as a rough approximation to some rather different kinds of situations, we can ask several questions: (1) Are different kinds of change distributed differentially in the population? (2) Do changes as we have measured them agree with the reasons people give when we ask them why they are better or worse off financially? (3) Do different kinds of changes have different effects on spending behavior? We will deal with the first two questions here. The third will be answered in Chapter 6 in a more complete analysis of the panel data.

Certain obvious patterns exist by definition. There cannot be changes in the income of wife or others when there are no such people in the unit.

Other patterns can easily be predicted. Changes in weeks worked accompanied by changes in earnings were most frequent in the construction industry, with mining and manufacturing second. The largest proportion of decreases in earnings were reported in agriculture, the smallest proportion of increases in construction. There were no significant differences by race. The more years of formal education, the fewer reports, relatively, of lower earnings and the more reports, relatively, of higher earnings. High school graduates did not report as high a proportion of increases as college men nor as large a proportion of decreases as those with still less education, hence, the high school graduates were more likely to report no change.

Unfavorable financial events are more likely to come as a surprise. People whose earnings dropped but who continued to work the same number of weeks were not as unpleasantly surprised as those whose earnings dropped and who worked fewer weeks.

Men reported increases more frequently and women reported decreases more frequently. Craftsmen, operatives, laborers, and service workers were more likely to report changes in weeks of work along with their changes in earnings.[6]

Finally, Table 3-8 gives some of the main types of income change as a proportion of those within each age group. In general the patterns shown in this table are reasonable. However, the very large fraction of those 65 or older reporting lower earnings without working fewer weeks indicates that older people shift to worse jobs, experience a drop in self-employment income, or lose extra work more frequently than one might expect.[7]

Relation of Types of Income Change to Expressed
Reasons for Being Better or Worse Off

Table 3-9 shows that the new code created out of the income detail in two interviews to characterize types of income change contains some information that is different from what is elicited by merely asking people why they are better or worse off. Many people with very small

---

[6]The greater income variability of the unskilled, greater even than that of the self-employed, was noted by L. R. Klein and N. Liviatan in 1957 but the facts have been consistently ignored. See "The Significance of Income Variability on Savings Behaviour," *Bulletin of the Oxford University Institute of Statistics,* Vol. 19 (May 1957), pp. 151-160.

[7]For reasons people gave for their income changes from 1956 to 1957, see J. Morgan, "The Anatomy of Income Distribution," *Review of Economics and Statistics,* XLIV (August 1962), 270-83.

Table 3-8

PROPORTIONS WITHIN EACH AGE GROUP
REPORTING EACH OF THREE MAIN KINDS OF CHANGE IN HEAD'S EARNINGS
(Panel of 1059 spending units, 1960-1962)

| Age | Same number of weeks worked[a] | | | | Fewer weeks worked[a] | |
| | Higher earnings | | Lower earnings | | Lower earnings | |
	1959-60	1960-61	1959-60	1960-61	1959-60	1960-61
18-34	38	43	16	16	4	9
35-44	38	39	22	23	9	4
45-54	29	29	28	24	9	6
55-64	26	28	28	32	13	12
65 or older	13	10	61	66	14	10
All ages	29	30	30	32	10	8

[a]Number of full or part time weeks worked was the same in each year.

Note: Numbers of cases on which proportions are based range from 177 to 273.

Table 3-9

REPORTED REASONS FOR SPENDING UNIT BEING BETTER OR WORSE OFF FINANCIALLY,
WITHIN KINDS OF INCOME CHANGE, 1960-1961

(Panel of 1059 spending units, 1960-1962)

| | Cases | Reasons for spending unit head's income change, 1960-1961 | | | | | | |
| | | Head's earnings higher | | Head's earnings lower | | Head's earnings same[b] | | |
		Worked no more weeks	Worked more weeks	Worked no fewer weeks	Worked fewer weeks	Total SU income higher	Total SU income lower	Total SU income same[b]
Better off	61	80	84	42	26	69	56	71
Better pay	26	39	37	9	6	31	#	38
Higher income from self-employment or property	8	8	8	12	1	9		6
More work, hence more income	8	11	21	4	9	11		3
Increased contributions from outside SU	2	1	0	4	4	0		3
Decreased expenses	4	4	5	4	1	2		4
Better asset-debt position	11	14	10	7	4	14		16
Other reasons	2	3	3	2	1	2		1
Worse off	39	30	33	41	68	42	48	42
Lower pay	3	1	1	3	5	2		2
Lower income from self-employment or property	4	2	0	9	6	7		0
Less work, hence less income	12	8	17	10	42	5		8
Higher prices	6	7	4	5	1	7		13
Higher taxes	1	1	0	1	2	4		1
Increased expenses	9	8	8	8	1	15		12
Worse asset-debt position	3	3	3	4	7	2		4
Other reasons	1	0	0	1	4	0		2
No reasons given	30	25	16	41	30	27	33	27
Number of cases	1018	321	67	335	82	55	27	131
Per cent of subsample	100	31	7	33	8	5	3	13

Too few cases to report data.

[a] Total adds to more than 100 per cent because more than one reason, including offsetting reasons, was recorded. The question was, "We are interested in how people are getting along financially these days. Would you say that you and your family are better off or worse off financially than you were a year ago? Why is that?"

[b] Income did not increase or decrease by 5 per cent or more.

changes in spending unit income report better pay, and apparently a substantial number with lower earnings do not give lower pay as a reason for being worse off financially.

An examination of cases of apparent discrepancies between the inferred and expressed reasons for change revealed a variety of complexities that made sense upon examination. It also left the impression that the coding of types of income change worked well for ordinary families, but not so well for farmers and self-employed businessmen. For them, their own summarization of change in status and the reasons for it may well be more reliable.

Persistence, Uniqueness, or Reversal of Changes

Are some kinds of changes more likely to be reversed the next year than others? This question is particularly crucial since errors in reporting of any one item, particularly for the central year, would lead to apparent reversals of direction. Actually, Table 3-10 shows some reversals, but also a substantial number of changes that repeat themselves in the second pair of years. Finally, it shows that only a very small fraction of the panel had an income that changed by less than 5 per cent for both pairs of years.

When we remember that some of the changes in income are the results of voluntary decisions by families desiring more money, or perhaps more leisure or more children, the whole concept of income as a simple exogenous variable in the household sector begins to seem invalid. As yet there appears to be no way to distinguish voluntary from involuntary changes in income, though as we have said, changes in the wife's income would seem more likely to be voluntary, and change in income without employment change would seem somewhat less involuntary than change in income accompanied by change in employment.

Persistence of change or reversal can also be examined by asking whether surprises (reported changes in financial situation differing from beginning-of-year expectations) tend to be followed by reversals. Table 3-11 seems to show more persistence than reversals, particularly in surprises. About one-fourth of the people who found themselves better off than expected in early 1961 had the same pleasant surprise in early 1962, and over one-third of those who found themselves worse off than expected in early 1961 also found themselves worse off than expected in early 1962. Perhaps general optimism or pessimism persists, so that optimists continue to be surprised by bad things, and

Table 3-10

REASONS FOR INCOME CHANGE FROM 1959 TO 1960, BY REASONS FOR INCOME CHANGE
FROM 1960 TO 1961

(Panel of 1059 spending units, 1960-1962)

Reasons for income change from 1960 to 1961	All panel units	Reasons for income change from 1959 to 1960									
		Head's earnings higher		Head's earnings lower		Head's earnings same[a]		Earnings of head and wife same[a]			Change N.A.
		Same/ fewer weeks	More weeks worked	Same more weeks	Fewer weeks worked	Wife has more	Wife has less	Total SU income higher	Total SU income lower	Total SU income same	
Head's earnings higher											
1. Worked same or fewer weeks	321	91	28	111	9	10	9	11	7	44	1
2. Worked more weeks	67	12	9	3	31	1	2	0	2	3	4
Head's earnings lower											
3. Worked same or more weeks	335	97	14	159	28	4	1	3	0	19	10
4. Worked fewer weeks	82	18	17	14	18	1	0	2	9	0	3
Head's earnings same											
5. Wife has more	25	11	0	2	0	5	2	0	0	5	0
6. Wife has less	17	2	2	6	4	2	0	0	0	1	0
Earnings of head and wife the same											
7. Total SU income more	32	8	4	4	1	0	0	1	3	10	1
8. Total SU income less	10	3	0	0	4	0	0	2	0	1	0
Total spending unit income unchanged[a]	131	61	16	11	3	2	5	3	1	29	0
Not ascertained	42	9	2	10	5	0	1	1	2	1	11
All panel units	1059	312	92	320	103	25	20	23	24	113	30

[a]Income did not increase or decrease by 5 per cent or more.

Table 3-11

FULFILLMENT OF 1961 PERSONAL FINANCIAL EXPECTATIONS, BY FULFILLMENT OF 1960 EXPECTATION

(Percentage distribution of a panel of 1059 spending units, 1960-1962)

Fulfillment in 1962 of personal financial expectations expressed early in 1961	All cases	Fulfillment in 1961 of personal financial expectations expressed early in 1960						
		Better than expected	Expected improvement confirmed	Expectations of no change confirmed	Expected worsening confirmed	Uncertainty in either year	Worse than expected	Not ascertained
Better than expected	21	4	3	5	1	1	7	0
Expected improvement confirmed	15	3	6	1	0	1	4	0
Expectations of no change confirmed	28	4	1	13	1	1	8	0
Expected worsening confirmed	1	0	0	0	0	0	1	0
Uncertainty in either year	6	1	0	2	0	1	2	0
Worse than expected	28	3	4	6	1	1	13	0
Not ascertained	1	0	0	0	0	0	1	0
Per cent of sample	100	15	14	27	3	5	36	0

Note: In early 1960 and 1961 the question about expectations was, "Now looking ahead--do you think that a year from now you people will be better off financially, or worse off, or just about the same as now?"

In early 1961 and 1962 the question about fulfillment was, "We are interested in how people are getting along financially these days. Would you say that you and your family are better off or worse off financially than you were a year ago?"

pessimists by good things. Of course, those who expect things to stay the same are the most likely to persist in this view, and to be right.

One implication of this tendency not to expect reversals is that there are very few people in any sample who can be described on the basis of their reported income change and expectations, as having had an unusually high or unusually low income last year. In early 1961 only 2 per cent said they were making more than a year ago but expected to be worse off a year from now. And at the same time only 6 per cent reported making less, but expected to be better off ''a year from now.''

Finally, there is a tendency for people to expect good things rather than bad, so that income decreases are more likely to be unexpected than decreases. In all three reinterviews, 1956-57, 1959-60 and 1960-61, it was the decreases in income that were the most likely to be unexpected. Table 3-12 summarized the results. The later panel also reinforced the earlier finding that there was very little if any correlation between a high current income and experience of unexpected increases.[8]

Summary

Perhaps our most startling finding is the very large number of changes in income not associated with unemployment or with recovery from unemployment that are not reversed in the following year. Secondly, there appear to be a substantial number of spending units where there is a change in income even though there is no change in the head's earnings. The evidence of the effects of wife's earnings on spending is contradictory, or at least varied. Our preliminary work seems to indicate that the fraction of income spent on durables and consumer investments is unaffected, but other studies seem to show effects on detailed budget allocations, say for clothes and transportation. The crucial question is the effect on saving, which is discussed in Chapter 6.

[8]J. N. Morgan, ''The Anatomy of Income Distribution,'' *op. cit.*, p. 278.

Table 3-12

EXPECTED AND UNEXPECTED INCOME CHANGES FROM THREE REINTERVIEWS

	1956-57	1959-60	1960-61
Increased			
Unexpectedly	17	15	20
As expected	28	19	18
Decreased			
Unexpectedly	15	15	10
As expected	3	5	5
No change or not ascertained	37	46	47
Total	100	100	100
Number of spending units reinterviewed	817	1434	1232

[a]Actual changes were measured by questions about income change reported and anticipated in the 1957 and 1958 Surveys. In the 1960, 1961, and 1962 Surveys, the question in the prior interview asked whether the respondent expected the spending unit to be better or worse off financially a year from now and the reinterview asked whether more or less money was being made.

Source: J. Morgan, "Anatomy of Income Distribution," The Review of Economics and Statistics, Vol. XLIV, No. 3 (August 1962), p. 278, and the 1960, 1961, and 1962 Surveys of Consumer Finances.

Chapter 4

Fulfillments of Consumer Buying Plans*

The main question to be investigated at this point is whether or not the predictive performance of a buying intention can be improved by relating this intention to other information about the consumer. A very specific kind of underlying relationship is hypothesized to connect these variables: it is a fulfillment relationship which we shall specify and try to estimate. A body of knowledge on the predictive quality of buying intentions and attitudinal variables has been built up in a number of studies based upon a single survey, or upon aggregative time series data.[1] The kind of test we propose to carry out is not so much a test of an explanatory variable but rather more a test of an explanatory relationship. Although there have been pioneering studies in this direction, several new ideas can be tried out in this study because of the availability of reinterview data in detail.[2]

*This study was designed and written by Richard F. Kosobud.

[1]Several representative studies may be cited: these studies in turn contain valuable references. T. G. Flechsig, "Anticipating Consumer Purchases of Durable Goods," *Proceedings of the Business and Economics Statistics Section of the American Statistical Association 1962*, pp. 152-57; F. T. Juster, "Predictive Value of Consumer's Union Spending Intentions Data," *The Quality and Economic Significance of Anticipations Data* (Princeton: Princeton University Press, 1960); E. Mueller, "Ten Years of Consumer Attitude Surveys: Their Forecasting Record," *Journal of the American Statistical Association*, LVIII (December 1963), 899-917; A. Okun, "The Value of Anticipations Data in Forecasting National Product," *The Quality and Economic Significance of Anticipations Data* (Princeton: Princeton University Press, 1960).

[2]I want to acknowledge a debt to the early studies of J. B. Lansing and S. B. Withey, Consumer Anticipations: Their Use in Forecasting Consumer Behavior," *Studies in Income and Wealth*, Vol. XVII (New York: National Bureau of Economic Research, 1954); and L. R. Klein and J. B. Lansing, "Decisions to Purchase Consumer Durable Goods," The Journal of Marketing, (October 1955), XX No. 2 109-32.

Repeated interviews with the same respondent such as occurred the 1961 and 1962 Surveys of Consumer Finances provide data indispensable to the purposes of this study. The battery of attitudinal questions developed at the Survey Research Center was asked of the consumer at each interview making information available on the sequence of attitudes, buying plans, and subsequent decisions. Respondents were asked about their buying plans for three commodity groups: cars, additions and repairs to housing units, and other major durables.[3] In particular, they were asked about the dollar amounts of their buying plans for these three groups and in the reinterview a year later they were asked about their dollar expenditures for these items.

What we propose to do with these data may be outlined in a series of steps through which the research proceeded.

1. At the first step buying plans were treated as a dependent variable in order to find out to what extent they depended upon other subjective and objective variables. A large unexplained variation in buying plans was found which led to the conclusion that buying plans were largely exogenous (at present).

2. At the second step, consumer buying plans were treated as an independent variable and their accuracy in predicting expenditures in a single cross section was appraised. It may be reported that buying plans revealed serious predictive imperfections: namely an overestimation of actual expenditures and a low degree of explanatory power (correlation coefficient).

3. Having uncovered serious predictive errors, the third step was undertaken. The deviation in dollars between expenditure and plan was related to the deviation between the expected and the realized value of other variables; i.e., a fulfillment relationship was specified and estimated. Measurement considerations became quite important at this step, and several innovations,

---

[3]The category "other major durables" includes as a group items such as a refrigerator, furniture, stove, washing machine, television set, etc., but excludes hobby items such as cameras.

such as the direct measurement of unanticipated events, were attempted.

4. In the final step, several very preliminary attempts to develop forecasting equations from fulfillment relationships were carried out.

It will be convenient and worthwhile to present these topics in the order of the outline.

Some Factors Influencing Buying Plans

Buying plans have been treated as one among a number of related expectations, and one which is formed relatively late "when the underlying sentiment has already been somewhat crystallized."[4] In this model buying plans are formed after other expectations and are dependent on them. Also buying plans for a commodity have been treated as a conditional forecast (or strategy) which depend upon a number of factors such as (a) the recent history of the consumer unit, (b) expectations of the values of variables external to the unit, (c) an appraisal of the existing inventory of the commodity, and (d) buying plans for other commodities.[5] These theoretical insights may be represented below in a diagram in which the flow of causation among the variables is indicated by arrows.[6] Consider, for example, the formation of buying plans for a car (see Diagram 4-1). This formulation could apply to economic units other than consumers and to commodities other than cars. In fact, it may be pointed out that the model may be more applicable to government and business units which have formal planning requirements. Against this view it may be argued that consumers who desire price and quality information may obtain it only at some cost. Therefore,

---

[4]George Katona, *The Powerful Consumer* (New York: McGraw-Hill Book Co., 1960) p. 63.

[5]Various formulations may be found in F. T. Juster, "Predictive Value of Consumer's Union Spending Intentions Data," *The Quality and Significance of Anticipations Data* (Princeton: Princeton University Press, 1960); H. Theil, *Economic Forecasts and Policy* (Amsterdam: North-Holland Publishing Co., 1958); and J. Tobin, "On the Predictive Value of Consumer Intentions and Attitudes," *Review of Economics and Statistics*, (February 1959). XLI, No. 1.

[6]Theil, *op. cit.*, p. 20.

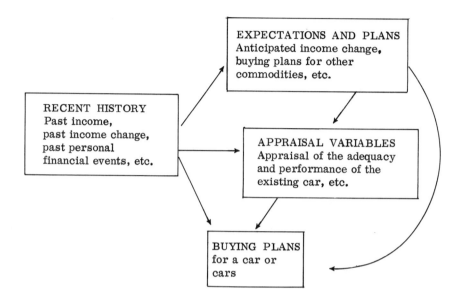

Diagram 4.1   Formation of Buying Plans.

a buying plan may indicate that the consumer has satisfied himself with respect to these data; that is, he has solved his problem and may not reopen the question unless something intervenes. The buying plan may indicate that the consumer is involved in related actions such as building up liquid assets to make down payments. In the face of uncertainty the buying plan may represent some type of calculation of the most probable course of action. In view of these considerations there seems to be no a priori reason for treating consumer buying plans as differing essentially from other anticipatory data.

That buying plans are associated with the current level of income may be noted in Table 4-1 in which buying plans for the next twelve months expressed early in 1961 for three commodity groups are related to 1960 total consumer unit income.[7] Buying plans for

[7]Consumer units were considered to have a buying plan for purposes of this study if they answered that they definitely would, or probably would, or might make expenditures for a commodity during the next twelve months or so and if they were able to indicate a dollar amount. The respondents were asked (in the case of cars): "Do you people expect to buy a car during the next twelve months or so?" (If yes) "How much do you think you will pay for it?"

TABLE 4-1

DOLLAR AMOUNT OF BUYING PLANS OF PANEL CONSUMER UNITS FOR THREE COMMODITIES, BY INCOME GROUP

(Percentage of 1059 spending units)

Buying plans for each commodity group as reported early in 1961[a]	All consumer units	Under $3000	Total spending unit income in 1960				
			$3000 to 4999	$5000 to 7499	$7500 to 9999	$10,000 to 14,999	$15,000 or more
Per cent of consumers planning to buy a car							
No plans	85	94	86	80	76	82	80
Plans to spend less than $2000	7	5	7	8	6	11	4
Plans to spend $2000 or more	8	1	7	12	18	7	16
	100	100	100	100	100	100	100
Per cent of consumers planning to spend for addition and repairs to housing units							
No plans	72	88	75	70	56	59	68
Plans to spend less than $500	17	9	16	18	20	24	12
Plans to spend $500 or more	12	3	9	12	24	17	20
	100	100	100	100	100	100	100
Per cent of consumers planning to buy other major durables							
No plans	77	91	84	74	64	62	68
Plans to spend less than $200	10	5	7	14	13	12	8
Plans to spend $200 or more	13	4	5	12	23	26	24
	100	100	100	100	100	100	100
Per cent of panel	100	23	20	26	16	11	4

[a] A few consumer units for whom buying plan information was not available were classified as not having buying plans.

additions and repairs were expressed by the highest proportion of panel members, about 30 per cent. Buying plans for other major durables were expressed by 23 per cent, and buying plans for new and used cars by 15 per cent of the panel. The proportion of consumer units expressing plans increased steadily with 1960 income up to the highest income class in which it decreased, significantly, for additions and repairs and other major durables. It may be that consumers with high income do not bother, in general, with buying plans. They may not, for example, have to plan to meet down payment requirements. The proportion of consumer units planning higher dollar amounts of expenditures also increases with income. In order to approach closer to the multivariate model for the formation of buying plans sketched previously, a number of regression equations were estimated by least squares methods. In these equations measures of some of the variables that may affect buying plans were introduced.

The significance of spending unit total income in the formation of buying plans is maintained in the more multivariate results presented in Table 4-2 for 863 panel members who reported data on all variables. Spending units which did not report owning a car (largely units with older heads) were omitted from this portion of the study in order to provide a better test of a variable measuring the age of the existing car. Descriptions of explanatory variables are given in the stub of Table 4-2. Regression coefficients for any single explanatory variable may be read across the row. Standard errors of the regression coefficients are given in parentheses. Note that the first two columns present alternative equations for cars.

Income in 1960 exhibits a higher slope coefficient (.2) in the equation determining buying plans for cars than in the equations for the other commodities. The significant positive intercepts are consistent with an interpretation of nonlinearity in the underlying relationship, a nonlinearity which takes the form of a slope coefficient that decreases as income increases.[8]

[8]Other interpretations of the positive intercepts are possible, it may be noted. If the purpose of the study were to estimate the form of the relationship more accurately, several alternatives to the model linear in the variables would seem worth pursuing. A conditional probability analysis has been developed by Guy Orcutt, Martin Greenberger, John Korbel, and Alice Rivlin, *Microanalysis of Sociometric Systems: A Simulation Study* (New York: Harper, 1961) and a limited dependent variable model by J. Tobin, "Estimation of Relationships for Limited Dependent Variables," *Econometrica*, XXVI, No. 1 (January, 1958).

TABLE 4-2

REGRESSIONS OF BUYING PLANS ON EXPLANATORY VARIABLES

(For 863 panel spending units)

Variables in the relationship	Buying plans expressed early in 1961 in dollars by commodity group (dependent variable)			
	Private passenger automobile	Private passenger automobile	Additions and repairs to housing units	Other major durables
Regression number	1	2	3	4
Constant term	203.727 (24.000)	218.290 (23.000)	317.862 (17.000)	163.545 (22.000)
Total 1960 consumer unit income (in dollars)	.208 (.054)	.160 (.080)	.081 (.036)	.076 (.016)
Expect to be better off financially? (scaled)[a]	-32.824 (13.582)	-26.134 (13.272)	-12.243 (9.407)	.557 (4.064)
Income change from 1959 to 1960 (scaled)[b]	-3.742 (21.666)	19.074 (19.874)	29.976 (14.958)	17.046 (6.245)
Buying plans for a car (in dollars)			-.020 (.024)	.029 (.010)
Buying plans for additions and repairs (in dollars)	-.041 (.049)			.016 (.015)
Buying plans for other durables (in dollars)	.326 (.114)		.087 (.079)	
Age of head of spending unit (scaled)[c]	8.964 (21.149)		-20.865 (14.514)	-17.046 (6.245)
Model year of car owned at beginning of the period (last two digits of year of model)		-39.574 (9.471)		
Correlation coefficient	.212	.264	.169	.302

[a]The number 1 was assigned if the respondent anticipated a better personal financial situation, 3 if the same, 5 if worse, and 8 if uncertain.

[b]The number 1 was assigned if the respondent reported more money in 1960 than in 1959, 3 if about the same, and 5 if less.

[c]1=18-24, 2=25-34, 3=35-44, 4=45-54, 5=55-64, 6=65 and over.

The consumer's expectations about his personal financial situation a year later (1961) were significantly related to his buying plans for cars but not to buying plans for other commodities. This anticipatory variable has been found to be highly correlated with income anticipations. It was scaled as a variable in such a way that the negative sign of the coefficient indicates favorable anticipations are associated with buying plans for cars.[9] Past income change was significantly related to buying plans for additions and repairs and for other major durables but not for cars. The variable was so scaled that an increase in current over past income was directly associated with buying plans for these commodities.[10] This finding suggests that buying plans for cars, which were on the average of a larger dollar amount than buying plans for the other commodities, depended on income anticipations whereas buying plans for the other commodities depended on past income changes.

Interrelationships among buying plans for different commodities are suggested by the coefficients of buying plan variable measured in dollar amounts introduced into the equations as right-hand variables.[11] Without additional information on anticipated income and price changes, it is not possible in this way to measure whether buying plans for cars complement or substitute for buying plans for additions and repairs. It is useful, however, to have a measure of

---

[9]The question was: "Now looking ahead—do you think that a year from now you people will be better off financially, or worse off, or just about the same?" Answers were coded 1 if the respondent anticipated a better personal financial situation, 3 if the same, 5 if worse, and 8 if uncertain. Although these numbers were assigned prior to this study they seemed close enough to our objectives to be retained. An alternative coding would have been to assign 0 or 1 to answers for each catagory but such coding would have required a fairly expensive data processing step.

[10]The question was: "Are you people making as much money now as you were a year ago, or more or less?" The assignment of numbers to these answers was 1 if less income was being made, 3 if the same, and 5 if more. These answers were coded for purposes other than those of this study; however, the numbers assigned seemed usable.

[11]Buying plans for various commodities should probably be treated as jointly dependent variables, and not as solely dependent variables as we have treated them. To the extent that buying plans are jointly dependent we cannot claim that our estimates of coefficients are consistent; however, the estimates may be said to be efficient around a biased value.

their association to compare with reported expenditures. Buying plans for cars and for other major durables were positively, and significantly, associated in the cross section. Plans for cars and for additions and repairs reveal a negative association; however, the coefficients cannot be taken to be different from zero with much confidence.

The coefficient associated with age is clearly nonsignificant in the equation for buying plans for cars. It is negative and more significant for additions and repairs, and negative and highly significant for other major durables.

A direct appraisal of stocks of the commodity on the part of the spending unit at the beginning of the period was not available, valuable as the appraisal would be. In lieu of the consumer's appraisal of his existing car, an indicator of the model year of the existing car was introduced into the equation. The coefficient was negative and highly significant indicating that the older his car the more frequently a consumer expressed buying plans for a new or a used car and the higher the dollar amounts of such plans. Hence, this variable may capture some elements of the replacement demand for cars. It fails to capture, however, the demand of a spending unit with a new car and an increased desire for a yet newer car.[12]

Our specification of buying plan relationships is not complete. A number of important variables relating to the recent history of the consumer and to his anticipations ought to be introduced in further work. The relatively low correlation coefficients may be due in part to this incomplete specification. More complete specification of the buying plan relationship may reduce the unexplained variation, but for the present we must conclude that buying plans contribute information not available in other variables.[13]

---

[12]A discussion of changing desires attributable to changing consumption levels may be found in G. Katona, *op. cit.*, pp. 130-37.

[13]This conclusion seems consistent with that of F. G. Adams, *Consumer Attitudes, Buying Plans and Purchases of Durable Goods: A Principle Components Approach*, Research Monograph No. 1, Economic Research Services Unit, University of Pennsylvania, 1962.

Predictive Accuracy of Buying Plans

A joint distribution of panel members by the simple fulfillment or nonfulfillment of a buying plan reveals the most dramatic type of predictive imperfections (Table 4-3). The most frequent imperfection is the one in which respondents did not report buying plans but in the reinterview twelve months later did report expenditures. About 20 per cent of spending units who did not report plans to buy a car did report the purchase of a car at the time of the reinterview. For other major durables the proportion of "unexpected purchases" is about 27 per cent and for addition and repairs the proportion is about 25 per cent. In absolute numbers it is clear that for cars and other major durables the number of nonplanners who made expenditures is greater than the number of planners who made expenditures. This is not true for additions and repairs where the number of planners and nonplanners who made expenditures is about the same.[14]

Another discrepancy between plan and fulfillment is revealed by those spending units that reported buying plans but did not report expenditures by the reinterview date. In the case of cars the proportion of planners who reported this predictive "error" is about 47 per cent. The proportion declines to 43 per cent in the case of other major durables and to 34 per cent in the case of additions and repairs. Looked at another way, spending units fulfilled plans to make expenditures for additions and repairs most frequently and plans to buy cars least frequently. Buying plans for addition and repair expenditures thus exhibited the best predictive performance in terms of this first simple test. It is unlikely that the difference in predictive performance can be attributed to the amount of expenditures alone (the mean addition and repair expenditure was lower than the mean car expenditure). The better performance of addition and repair buying plans may be due to the less postponable

---

[14]Considerable interest has been expressed in the group which does not report buying plans but later reports expenditures. It is possible to treat them as a separate group, T. G. Flechsig, *op. cit.*, p. 157, and George Katona, *The Powerful Consumer*, p. 171. It is also possible to treat them in a symmetrical way with spending units who report dollar expenditures larger than planned. We shall experiment with both approaches.

TABLE 4-3

JOINT DISTRIBUTION OF CONSUMER BUYING PLANS AND ACTUAL EXPENDITURES DURING 1961 FOR THREE COMMODITIES

(Percentage of 1059 spending units)

Reported expenditures during 1961	Buying plans expressed early in 1961								
	For a car			For other major durables			For additions and repairs		
	Planners	Non-planners	Total	Planners	Non-planners	Total	Planners	Non-planners	Total
For a car									
Buyers	8	17	25						
Nonbuyers	7	68	75						
Total	15	85	100						
For other major durables									
Buyers				13	21	34			
Nonbuyers				10	56	66			
Total				23	77	100			
For additions and repairs									
Spenders							19	18	37
Nonspenders							10	53	63
Total							29	71	100

nature of these expenditures although we need more evidence here. Up to this point we have pretty much confirmed the results of prior studies.[15] Our data, however, enable us to take a new step.

We know more about buying plans and expenditures than is revealed in Table 4-3; we know the dollar amounts of these variables. A tendency to underfulfill the dollar amount of buying plans (or to overestimate the dollar amount of expenditures) was observed for all three commodity groups and may be shown in tabular format in the case of buying plans for additions and repairs to houses. If we consider cases along the diagonal of Table 4-4 to be exact dollar fulfillment, then the 49 cases above the diagonal indicate overestimation and the 15 cases below the diagonal indicate underestimation of planned expenditures.

The predictive errors exhibited by dollar amounts of buying plans and subsequent expenditures may be investigated more systematically by means of an accuracy analysis model. Consider a descriptive model

$$(1) \quad c_i = a_0 + a_1 \, c_i^e \qquad (i = 1, \ldots, 1059 \text{ panel members})$$

in which c represents actual dollar expenditures during period t for cars by panel member i, and c_i^e represents dollar expenditures expected to be made or planned at the beginning of period t.[16] Perfect prediction of the level of expenditures may be defined as $a_0 = 0$, $a_1 = 1$, and a correlation coefficient of unity. A slope coefficient less than unity may be interpreted as a systematic overestimation of the level of actual expenditures. For this interpretation we assume individuals in the panel to be interchangeable with respect to the dollar amounts of buying plans and subsequent expenditures.

Should an accuracy analysis of buying plans be carried out only

---

[15] C. Lininger, E. Mueller, and H. Wyss, "Some Uses of Panel Studies in Forecasting the Automobile Market," *Proceedings of the Business and Economics Section of the American Statistical Association*, September 1957, pp. 409-21.

[16] Period t refers to the twelve-month period following the interview data. By use of the twelve-month period, the problem of seasonality is avoided: U.S. Bureau of the Census, *Current Populations Reports*, Series P-65, No. 1, "Consumer Buying Intentions," March 12, 1963, p. 2. A fresh problem is encountered, however, in that consumers may act upon a shorter horizon: T. G. Flechsig, *op. cit.*, p. 157.

TABLE 4-4

JOINT DISTRIBUTION OF AMOUNT OF BUYING PLANS AND ACTUAL ADDITION AND REPAIR EXPENDITURES DURING 1961
FOR 201 PLANNERS AND BUYERS

(Percentage of 201 spending units)

Reported dollar amount of expenditures for additions and repairs during 1961	Planned dollar amount of expenditures for additions and repairs during 1961						
	$1-49	$50-99	$100-199	$200-499	$500-999	$1000 or more	Total
$1-49	2	2	3	3	1	2	13
$50-99	0	1	6	5	0	1	13
$100-199	0	1	6	6	5	2	20
$200-499	0	0	3	10	4	3	20
$500-999	0	0	1	5	7	6	19
$1000 or more	0	0	0	1	4	10	15
Total	2	4	19	30	21	24	100

for those spending units which planned and subsequently made expenditures? Or should an accuracy analysis be carried out for the entire panel? On the one hand, arguments have been advanced for treating combinations of planners and nonplanners and fulfillers and nonfulfillers as different groups with possibly different consumer personalities. For example, the group of consumers who do not express plans but who subsequently buy may be of interest because they make up a large fraction of all buyers. They may tend to be impulsive buyers or they may tend to have other personality traits which could be discovered by studying them separately. On the other hand, it is possible to view a consumer's expressed buying plan as a statement that the probability of his buying exceeds some threshhold probability unique to him. Consumers, in this view, take their place in a probability distribution of plans, and the probability of subsequently buying may be made to depend upon a number of variables.[17] This line of reasoning suggests that the panel be treated as a whole. We shall try both approaches.

The regressions of actual expenditures upon buying plans reveal in a more explicit way that the latter exhibited systematic predictive errors during 1961 except in the case of one subgroup and one commodity. Buying plans persistently overestimated actual expenditures as indicated by slope coefficients significantly less than unity in Table 4-5.[18] The positive, significant constant terms suggest that the finding of overestimation ought to be modified in the range of small values. The correlation coefficients are low and suggest that in no case can it be claimed that buying plans alone explained more than a quarter of the variation of actual expenditures.

For the entire panel, systematic overestimation of actual expenditures occurred more frequently in buying plans for cars and least frequently in plans for addition and repairs. For the subgroup of panel members who both planned and spent, buying plans were also characterized by predictive errors but in the case of cars and

---

[17] I am indebted to Professor Lester D. Taylor for calling my attention to this model based upon the discussion in J. Tobin, "On the Predictive Value of Consumer Intentions and Attitudes," *op. cit.*

[18] Juster has reported similar results in his study, "Predictive Value of Consumer's Union Spending Intentions Data," *op. cit.*, p. 269.

TABLE 4-5

PREDICTIVE ACCURACY OF CONSUMER BUYING PLANS FOR COMMODITY GROUPS AND SPENDING UNIT GROUPS

(Plans and expenditures measured in current dollars)

Variables in the accuracy analysis (in dollars)	Predictive accuracy by commodity for selected panel groups								
	Cars			Additions and repairs			Other durables		
	Entire panel	Planners and buyers	Panel with income over $7500	Entire panel	Planners and buyers	Panel with income over $7500	Entire panel	Planners and buyers	Panel with income over $7500
Regression number	5	6	7	8	9	10	11	12	13
Constant term	341.85 (10.50)	934.11 (118.00)	549.12 (66.00)	111.398 (45.00)	176.97 (72.72)	174.77 (49.67)	76.769 (8.0)	3.538 (30.000)	173.637 (10.000)
Buying plans for a car during 1961	.371 (.039)	.558 (.125)	.261 (.065)						
Buying plans for addition and repair expenditures during 1961				.473 (.035)	.676 (.077)	.686 (.064)			
Buying plans for other durables during 1961							.420 (.043)	1.110 (.141)	.216 (.090)
Correlation coefficient	.245	.480	.200	.412	.520	.500	.320	.555	.188
Number of panel consumer units	1059	85	325	1059	204	332	1059	138	332

additions and repairs the degree of overestimation of actual expenditures was less than that of the entire panel. For this subgroup in the case of other durables neither over- nor underestimation of actual expenditures on the part of buying plans was exhibited (regression 12). For panel members whose 1960 income was $7500 or more, somewhat divergent tendencies may be noted. The degree of overestimation increases in the case of cars and other major durables but remained about the same in the case of additions and repairs.

To the extent the magnitude of the slope coefficient is dependent upon variables which move over time but remain relatively fixed in a cross section (price, credit terms, the distribution of anticipations) a possible explanation of the difference between the predictive performance of buying plans over time and over the individuals of a cross section is revealed by our results. Shifts in the slope coefficients over time due to the influence of these variables could lead to a predictive record that is worse in aggregate tests than in cross section tests. The stability over time of the cross section coefficients thus becomes an interesting empirical question.

Other anticipatory data have been evaluated for predictive performance in a similar way. Hart has reported that a regression of railroad shippers' quarterly freight car requirements upon forecasts of these requirements, both variables measured in terms of the per cent change over the freight car requirements of four quarters ago, yielded a slope coefficient of 2 which indicated significant underestimation of the actual per cent change.[19] Consequently, consumer buying plans appear to have exhibited a different type of predictive error during the sample period than railroad shipper's forecasts.

Fulfillment Relationships

There is a limit to the information that can be obtained from the descriptive accuracy analysis model. The results are not

---

[19]A. G. Hart, "Quantitative Evidence for the Interwar Period on the Course of Business Expectations: A Revaluation of the Railroad Shipper's Forecast," *The Quality and Economic Significance of Anticipations Data* (Princeton: Princeton University Press, 1960), p. 212.

invariant to simple transformations of the variables. Additional progress may come by considering the reasons for deviations between planned and actual expenditures. A simple fulfillment relationship may be developed along the following lines. Major investment expenditures of the consumer are thought to be determined by expressed buying plans and unanticipated changes in other variables such as income and prices. A simple illustrative model may be written in linear form as follows:

$$(2) \quad c_i = a_0 + a_1 c_i^e + a_2 (y_i - y_i^e)$$

$$(i = 1, \ldots, 1059 \text{ panel members})$$

in which y_i^e represents the expected income flow for the period (anticipated prior to the period) and y_i represents the realized income flow. The coefficient a_2 cannot be directly interpreted as a marginal propensity to spend out of unanticipated income. It would seem more useful to consider the coefficient to be a combination of (a) a coefficient measuring the speed of response of the consumer to unanticipated changes in income and (b) a coefficient representing the influence of income level. Consequently, the fulfillment relationship may be viewed as a highly simplified but useful account of complex consumer expenditure behavior.[20]

If c_i^e is subtracted from both sides of equation (2), a fulfillment relationship is obtained in convenient form for estimation purposes:

$$(3) \quad c_i - c_i^e = a_0 + (a_1 - 1) c_i^e + a_2 (y_i - y_i^e)$$

$$(i = 1, \ldots, 1059 \text{ panel members}).$$

A noteworthy feature of this model is that conventional variables and attitudinal variables are combined in a behavioral relationship. Deviations between actual and planned expenditures are made to depend upon unanticipated movements or deviations between actual and expected values of explanatory variables. Measurement of these deviations would appear to present critical problems. Ordinarily

---

[20]A development of the ideas underlying the model in the case of business plans is given in F. Modigliani and K. J. Cohen, *The Role of Anticipations and Plans in Economic Behavior and Their Use in Economic Analysis and Forecasting* (Urbana: University of Illinois, 1961).

one is forced to make some indirect estimate of deviations between anticipated and realized values but the panel character of our data present opportunities to measure them more directly. It will be worthwhile to explain these measurement practices in some detail.

The dependent variable was prepared by subtracting the planned dollar amount the respondent reported early in 1961 from the dollar expenditure amount he reported early in 1962.[21] A measure of price movements unanticipated by consumers during 1961 was prepared by comparing the respondent's anticipations of the rate of change of the price level at the time of the first interview and at the time of the reinterview. If anticipations of the respondent changed so that a lower rate of increases of prices was anticipated, an arbitrary low number was assigned to the variable. It anticipations changed so that a relatively higher rate of increase of prices was anticipated, an arbitrary high number was assigned. Numbers intermediate in value were assigned to unchanged anticipations.[22] A change in anticipations may, for example, be brought about by a perceived change in the price level. A plausible hypothesis about the relation of this variable to the deviation between actual and planned car expenditures is that prices lower than anticipated—and by assumption the effective prices of cars—would be associated with unanticipated positive expenditures for a car; i.e., the constructed variable ought to exhibit a negative coefficient. It is also possible that expectations of a higher rate of increase of future prices could lead to unanticipated positive expenditures for automobiles. This variable, clearly, bristles with problems of interpretation.[23]

A measure of business conditions unanticipated by consumers during 1961 was prepared by comparing the respondent's

[21]In the case of purchase of or plans to buy two or more cars, the dollar value of the highest priced car was studied.

[22]A more exact account of the preparation of this variable together with sample sizes is given in Table 4-9. To the extent consumers revised their anticipations in both directions, an estimate of the response to variables which move over time may be obtained from one reinterview. It may be noted than when reinterviewed 20 per cent of the panel reported anticipations of a lower rate of increase of prices than when first interviewed.

[23]In this approach it will be convenient to assume that prices anticipated at all future dates change in the same relative amount. This is equivalent, I believe, to assuming that the elasticity of price anticipations is unity.

anticipations in the first interview and in the reinterview of business conditions during the twelve months to come. A change in anticipations toward less favorable conditions was assigned an arbitrary low number. A change toward more favorable conditions was assigned an arbitrary high number. Among the reasons respondents frequently gave for anticipations of good or bad business conditions were anticipations of good or bad employment prospects. Consequently, a positive relation between this variable and unanticipated expenditures for cars seems plausible on a priori grounds.

A variable that was designed to measure unanticipated financial events was prepared by comparing the personal financial position as reported by the respondent at the end of 1961 with the anticipated financial position at the beginning of the period.[24] If the respondent's personal financial situation turned out to be less favorable than he had anticipated, an arbitrary large number was assigned. If the respondent's personal financial situation turned out to be more favorable than anticipated, an arbitrary small number was assigned. The reports consumers give about personal financial events have been found to be highly correlated with income changes. However, events that affect the balance sheet of consumer units may also enter into the variable; for example, an unanticipated illness which depletes liquid assets. In either case, we may reasonably expect a negative relation between this constructed variable and unanticipated expenditures.

By way of introducing these constructed variables we present, in Table 4-6, a conditional distribution of fulfillment of spending plans for a car and for additions and repairs within a measure of the fulfillment of consumer financial expectations for 1961. A comparatively small proportion of consumers who reported unfavorable events which surprised them fulfilled their buying plans for cars. The proportion of consumer units which did not fulfill addition and repair buying plans was also lower for this group.

A more complete specification of the fulfillment relationship may be estimated by incorporating the variables representing unanticipated changes in prices, business conditions, and financial

---

[24] It was found in an earlier study that unexpected income increases were reported more frequently by respondents who bought but did not report plans: Lansing and Withey, *op. cit.*, Table 43, p. 428.

TABLE 4-6

A CONDITIONAL DISTRIBUTION OF FULFILLMENT OF BUYING PLANS FOR 1961
WITHIN FULFILLMENT OF CONSUMER FINANCIAL EXPECTATIONS FOR 1961

(Percentage of 1059 spending units)

Fulfillment of spending plans during 1961	All units	Fulfillment of consumers' expectations about their financial situations during 1961				
		Better than expected	Improved, as expected	Same, as expected	Worse than expected	Not available or other combinations*
For cars						
Per cent of planners who bought	53	54	51	52	43	*
Per cent of nonplanners who bought	21	25	24	20	21	*
For additions and repairs						
Per cent of planners who bought	65	73	62	60	59	*
Per cent of nonplanners who bought	25	24	27	24	28	*
Per cent of panel	100	20	15	30	29	6

*This group contains those anticipating a worsening of their financial situation which was fulfilled during 1961. This group together with not available cases were too few to distribute.

situation into a linear regression model as sketched out earlier. Single equation least squares methods are appropriate in this model as the direction of influence ought to run from these unexpected events to unexpected expenditures.

In the case of fulfillment relationships for automobiles expenditures, estimates for the panel and for the subgroup of intenders and subsequent buyers are presented in the first two equations (which are arranged in columnar fashion) of Table 4-7. The coefficient of the buying plans variable $(a_1 - 1)$ is highly significant and negative as expected. If 1 is added to the coefficient for the equation for the entire panel a value is obtained (.345) which is consistent with the accuracy analysis results presented in Table 4-5. The comparable value for the subgroup (.539) is also consistent with prior results. The signs of the coefficients of the variable representing unanticipated price movements in the two equations are negative indicating that shifts in anticipations toward higher prices are associated with smaller expenditures than intended. The absolute value of the coefficient may not be too important in these first results in view of the crude scaling of the variable.

The signs of the coefficients associated with the variable representing unanticipated developments in business conditions is positive for the entire panel, as expected, but negative for the subgroup of intenders and subsequent buyers. The coefficients are small relative to their standard errors so that they cannot be considered to differ significantly from zero.[25]

The signs of the coefficients associated with unanticipated personal financial events are of the expected negative sign and significant in the case of the equation for the subgroup of intenders and buyers. Unanticipated financial or income events of an unfavorable character lead, in the case of the automobiles, to expenditures smaller than anticipated.

---

[25]Additional experiments were carried out with this variable for different subgroups of the panel. For a subgroup of older families this variable yielded a coefficient of the expected sign and significant at the conventional level. It is conceivable that for this older group a change in expectations about business conditions is more closely related to changes in perceived employment prospects and consequently to expenditures different from planned.

TABLE 4-7

FULFILLMENT RELATIONSHIPS FOR BUYING PLANS AND EXPENDITURES
FOR THREE COMMODITY GROUPS DURING 1961

Variables in the relationship	For cars		For additions and repairs		For other major durables	
	All panel members[a]	Members who intended and bought	All panel members[a]	Members who intended and bought	All panel members	All panel members
Regression number	14	15	16	17	18	19
Constant term	343.967 (39.611)	1744.867 (137.439)	220.753 (23.159)	541.288 (82.848)	140.554 (13.132)	157.248 (13.098)
Buying plans for the commodity (in dollars)	-.655 (.051)	-.461 (.150)	-.436 (.038)	-.330 (.083)	-.582 (.049)	-.589 (.049)
Changes in price expectations[b]	-44.512 (27.795)	-125.845 (94.090)	-20.720 (16.224)	-40.972 (56.570)	-6.128 (9.222)	-6.807 (9.190)
Changes in business condition expectations[b]	+4.933 (27.969)	-3.654 (103.217)	+14.664 (16.407)	+49.216 (61.336)	-1.721 (9.303)	-2.416 (9.283)
Unanticipated personal financial events[b]	+22.456 (19.197)	-151.108 (73.725)				-17.382 (6.362)
Reported change in income during 1961[b]			-24.630 (16.055)	-75.647 (52.838)	-18.877 (9.050)	
Correlation coefficient	.47	.49	.43	.34	.44	.44
Number of panel members	605	48	605	139	605	605

[a] All panel members who reported information.
[b] The scaling of these variables is explained in the preceding text.

Turning to the fulfillment relationships for additions and repairs, it may be noted from Table 4-7 that the coefficients of the buying plans variable are highly significant. While the coefficients of the variables representing unanticipated price movements have the expected sign, the confidence with which they can be taken to be different from zero in the case of additions and repairs is not great. It is possible that this very general price variable is less applicable to the diverse items included in the category additions and repairs. Nor may the coefficients associated with unanticipated developments in business conditions be taken to be different from zero with much confidence although the signs are as anticipated. Relatively more significant were the coefficients of the variable representing reported changes in income. This variable yielded about the same results as the variable representing unanticipated personal financial events with which it was positively correlated. A reported decrease in income during 1961 was associated with actual expenditures being less than planned for additions and repairs and for other major durables.

Consider the equations for other major durables. It did not appear worthwhile to distinguish the subgroup of intenders and buyers in the case of these widely different commodities which range from refrigerators to television sets: consequently, regressions number 18 and 19 present alternative models or structures for the entire panel reporting data. The signs of the coefficients (negative) associated with the variable representing unanticipated movements in prices are consistent with the a priori interpretation of this variable but the magnitudes of the coefficients are less than their standard errors. The coefficients of the variable representing unanticipated developments in business conditions have the "wrong" sign but their magnitude is clearly close to zero. A variable representing unanticipated personal financial events and a variable representing reported changes in income during 1961 exhibited significant coefficients of the expected sign. As both variables were scaled in about the same rough way, the similar magnitude of the coefficients in the last two equations suggest that the unexpected personal financial event that influenced the fulfillment of plans was frequently an unexpected change in income.

The estimated fulfillment relationships provide an explanation of the overestimation of actual car expenditures by buying plans during 1961 that was revealed by the accuracy analysis. It would appear that unanticipated unfavorable personal financial events—

which may be largely unanticipated unfavorable income events—provide part of the explanation of why actual expenditures were less than planned. That is, people, on the average, anticipated higher incomes than they received during 1961. Next in importance were unanticipated price increases.[26] Unanticipated developments in business conditions proved least significant in these preliminary efforts.

Further research is suggested in several areas.

1. In this study we have been fortunate in being able to make use of well-developed anticipatory data. The requirements of fulfillment models seem even more demanding in this respect. It seems worth investigating whether, for example, buying plans are formed in association with income anticipations expressed in dollar amounts.[27]

2. An additional variable which ought to prove of importance in a fulfillment model for cars is a variable representing the respondent's appraisal of the adequacy and the expected performance of his existing car. Other stock appraisal variables ought to be of value.

3. Finally it may be noted that the simple linear model into which we forced the fulfillment relationship seems inappropriate. Unanticipated events of a large magnitude may have a disproportionate influence upon unanticipated expenditures. The highly significant constant terms, all positive, are consistent with interpretations of nonlinear relationships. Despite these limitations, it seems worthwhile to show here how fulfillment models can be developed into forecasting relationships of potential value.

From Fulfillment Relationships
to Forecasting Equations

In a formal sense it is easy to illustrate how buying plans may be incorporated into an expenditure or forecasting relationship with

---

[26]It is of interest that expenditures for automobiles and parts during 1961 were below those of prior years. Price increases were reported during 1961 of a not inconsiderable amount. Some data are presented in Table 16, *Survey of Current Business*, July 1962, p. 15.

[27]Respondents were asked in the 1962 Survey of Consumer Finances (conducted early in 1962) for their expected 1962 income in dollar amounts. Most respondents were able to provide dollar amounts. This question was not asked in earlier surveys.

other variables. Buying plans may be added to both sides of the
fulfillment relationship so as to obtain (generally):

(4) $\quad c_{li} = c(c^e_j, y_{it} - y^e_{it}, \ldots)$

$$(i = 1, \ldots, 1059 \text{ panel members})$$

in which expenditures are made to depend upon plans and unanticipated movements of other variables entering into consumer expenditures. It is easy to recast our fulfillment relationships in this
form. All variables are scaled as before. Estimates of several
examples of the expenditure relation reveal that buying plans played
a highly significant and important role but that unanticipated developments as we have measured them contribute explanatory power,
and raise correlation coefficients to interesting levels (Table 4-8).

The variable representing unanticipated price movements is
negative in sign; however, it cannot be regarded as significantly
different from zero according to the conventional test. The variable
representing unanticipated developments in business conditions is of
the correct sign and significant at the one standard deviation level.
The variable representing unanticipated personal financial events is
of the correct sign, and becomes significant at the conventional level
in the equation for other major durables.

A significant positive association between expenditures for
additions and repairs and expenditures for other major durables is
revealed in regression 22. This cannot be taken as clear evidence
of complementarity, however, as we have not been able to cleanse
the data of the influence of other variables. It seems noteworthy
that this positive association between actual expenditures was also
revealed between planned expenditures for the two commodities.
There is no reason for the signs to be the same. It is easy to think
of situations in which plans are positively related because, for
example, the consumer anticipates an income increase while expenditures are negatively related because realized income fell short
of anticipated income. An indication of this is to be found in the
positive association which was found between buying plans for cars
and other major durables, whereas the association between actual
expenditures for these commodities is revealed to be negative in
Table 4-8.

If a more detailed measure of unanticipated income movements
were available, we should expect that the coefficient of a variable
measuring the level of 1961 income ought not to be significant in our

TABLE 4-8

EXPENDITURE RELATIONSHIPS INCORPORATING BUYING PLANS FOR THREE COMMODITIES
(For 863 panel spending units reporting data)

Independent variables in the relationship (Expenditure and intention variables in dollars)	Relationships for commodities during 1961		
	Expenditures for private passenger automobiles	Expenditures for additions and repairs to housing units	Expenditures for other major durables
Regression number	20	21	22
Constant term	419.467 (30.000)	-1.519 (15.000)	239.397 (10.000)
Expressed intentions or buying plan	.283 (.043)	.457 (.035)	.377 (.044)
Changes in price expectations	-16.274 (23.050)	-11.515 (13.246)	-5.531 (7.195)
Changes in expectations about business conditions	26.509 (23.339)	13.234 (13.441)	.372 (7.311)
Unanticipated personal financial events	-30.056 (19.451)	6.943 (11.206)	-18.600 (6.060)
Automobile expenditures during 1961		.021 (.019)	-.006 (.010)
Addition and repair expenditures during 1961	.078 (.054)		.035 (.017)
Other major durable expenditures during 1961	-.143 (.104)	.091 (.060)	
Total spending unit income during 1961	.168 (.049)	.097 (.028)	.014 (.015)
Age of head of consumer unit	-35.519 (25.418)	32.588 (14.664)	-23.529 (7.965)
Correlation coefficient	.298	.448	.361

specification. However, we have not used a sharp measure of unanticipated income. Nor have we been able to deal with consumers
who do not plan for one reason or another. Consequently, the highly
significant role of the level of 1961 income in the equation for cars
and for additions and repairs is of interest. It may be noted that the
income variable is not significant in the equation for other major
durable expenditures.

A variable representing age of the head of the consumer unit
proved significant in the case of additions and repairs, in which it
is positive, and in the case of other major durables in which it is
negative. In the case of addition and repair expenditures it may be
noted that age is correlated with home ownership, and home ownership is correlated with addition and repair expenditures so that the
positive association is plausible.

It is not claimed as yet that the models have been adequately
specified nor have the most suitable forms been estimated. The
final models do embody, however, both traditional and attitudinal
variables in a plausible framework for forecasting purposes. In an
actual application many additional steps would be required, of
course. For example, it would be necessary for the forecaster to
prepare an independent prediction of income and compare that prediction with anticipated income of consumers.

Summary

1. We have evidence that in addition to consumer income other
attitudinal variables as well as a variable representing the age of
the existing stock of the commodity (cars) play a role in the formation of buying plans.

2. An accuracy analysis of individual consumer buying plans
for three commodity groups revealed a persistent tendency for the
reported dollar value of plans to overestimate the subsequent dollar
expenditures during 1961. Buying plans all by themselves reveal
marked predictive imperfections.

3. A fulfillment relationship provided an explanation of the
deviation between actual expenditure and planned expenditure. The
unusually low levels of expenditures for cars during 1961 appears to
have been due to unexpected unfavorable income events and to a
lesser extent to unexpected unfavorable price changes and unexpected business developments which influenced consumers.

4. A framework for combining attitudinal and traditional variables becomes available in the development of fulfillment relationships into forecasting models. Consumer buying plans may be
"corrected" if consumer income anticipations, for example, deviate
from other predictions of income available to the forecaster.

TABLE 4-9

CHANGES IN RESPONDENT'S EXPECTATIONS,
EARLY 1961 TO EARLY 1962

	Number of panel members in each category	Coded
(1) About prices		
Higher than previously expected	242	5
Unchanged		
Higher next year	407	4
Constant	120	3
Lower next year	6	2
Lower than previously expected	223	1
Not available or don't know	6	Not in-cluded
	1059	
(2) About business conditions		
More optimistic	440	5
Same		
Good times ahead	294	4
Uncertain	12	3
Bad times ahead	12	2
Less optimistic	158	1
Not available or don't know	143	Not in-cluded
	1059	
(3) Fulfillment of personal financial expectations		
Not fulfilled, better off than expected	210	1
Fulfilled		
Better off	156	2
About the same	300	3
Worse off	20	4
Not fulfilled, worse off than expected	299	5
Not available or don't know	74	Not in-cluded
	1059	

The questions asked were:
(1) "Speaking of prices in general, I mean the prices of things you buy--do you think they will go up in the next year or go down, or stay where they are now?"
(2) "And how about a year from now, do you expect that in the country as a whole business conditions will be better or worse than they are at present or just about the same?"
(3) "Now looking ahead--do you think that a year from now you people will be better off financially, or worse off, or just about the same as now?" This question was asked early in 1961; then, early in 1962, the question to which it was compared was: "We are interested in how people are getting along financially these days. Would you say that you and your family are better off or worse off financially than you were a year ago?"

Chapter 5

Consumer Saving Relationships*

A Study Based Upon Saving and Income Variables

Measured Over Two Years

Estimates of the change in consumer saving induced by changes in income and assets make up useful pieces of positive knowledge. Quantitative studies with these estimates as their aim have encountered a number of problems, several of which are relevant to the objectives of this study.

a) In cross-section studies of saving behavior, the correlation coefficient has been found to be low indicating that this relationship is complex and that variables are present that have not yet been correctly specified.

b) Errors of measurement undoubtedly arise and may be important. We do not know, for example, how much reliance can be placed upon the memory of the respondent to provide useful information. It is always possible that a respondent questioned about income and saving flows answers in terms of a time period different from that which the investigator wanted to explore.

c) In estimating the influence of wealth upon saving behavior it has been difficult to isolate differences in saving preferences from the effects of assets, e.g., large assets may press downward on the saving rate, or they may be indicative of past saving habits. Other interpretations are possible. These problems lessen the power of quantitative studies to cast light upon important theoretical issues

*This study was designed by Richard F. Kosobud and John B. Lansing, and the chapter was written by Kosobud.

such as the direction and magnitude of any wealth effect upon the saving rate.

d) In previous studies it was not ascertained whether assets were inherited, received as gifts, or accumulated. Thus the investigators could not determine whether the assets reflected the saving behavior of the respondent or the donor.

e) There is a great deal of evidence that the saving behavior of certain groups (such as the self-employed and the retired) is quite distinctive. It seems likely that efforts to disaggregate the population further into groups in different situations will reveal other differences that are now obscured in aggregative data.

Data from repeated cross sections or a panel provide opportunities for a new approach to some of these problems. The point has already been made that it is possible during repeated interviews to ask the respondent many more questions than can be asked in one interview. A deeper advantage may also be claimed. By following families over a period of time we are able to obtain information on variables that change over this period. In the case of the current panel, questions were asked of respondents which enabled us to develop data on the sequence of events relating to anticipated income and, later, reported income. In this way, we began to exploit more fully some of the rich potentialities of panel data.

This accumulation of information will enable us to try some experiments in further disaggregation of the panel in an effort to disentangle the strands of some of the complicated issues mentioned previously. In particular we shall try to disentangle the effects of liquid assets upon the saving rate among groups believed to be in normal income situations, among groups anticipating different future income events, and among groups differing with respect to the receipt of gifts and inheritances.

Such advantages do not come without causing problems of their own. Repeated interviews are expensive and there are losses in the membership of the panel over time, losses which may cause biases. It will be important to treat these problems more fully later. At this point, however, it will be fitting to set forth some of the major ways which have been chosen to exploit these panel data.

Measures of two-year saving and two-year income were prepared from information obtained from 1059 spending units interviewed in the 1960 Survey of Consumer Finances and again in the 1961 and 1962 surveys. Consequently, relationships may be estimated in which key variables are defined over two years rather than over one year. A measure of the flow of saving over two years that is relatively comprehensive in its coverage of various types of transactions was prepared from the three interviews. Details on these measurement practices will be presented subsequently.

An effort was made to distinguish respondents in unusual income circumstances from those in more "normal" circumstances by studying the sequence of reported and anticipated incomes. We may expect saving behavior to differ between these groups.

The considerable body of information provided by panel members enables us, for example, to distinguish between those who did and those who did not receive gifts and inheritances. Thus panel data enabled us to carry further one of the unique advantages of cross-section data, and that is, the advantage of being able to disaggregate among the entire sample into subsamples more homogeneous with respect to economic situations. Prior to presenting the details of these techniques it will be worthwhile to set up the basic saving model which will be used in this study in a more explicit, formal way.

An Outline of the Saving Model

Among the variables we shall use to explain the rate of saving are those which vary from consumer unit to consumer unit, for example, current income, initial liquid asset holdings, life cycle, and selected attitudinal variables. Cross-section surveys have been considered uniquely suited to provide information on these variables. Another group of variables has often been treated as the same for all consumers, and fixed during the one time survey—those that vary over time such as prices (interest rates), tax rates, and Social Security eligibility criteria. We do not care to assume that these variables (for example, interest rates) are perceived in the same way by all consumer units. Nor does it appear quite satisfactory to assume that these variables were fixed over two years. These lines of inquiry cannot be pursued in this study and most of these variables are not dealt with in an explicit way. However, changes in income of the individual family over several years can be measured and in this respect a new step may be taken. A last group of variables may be said to vary from consumer unit to consumer unit due to differ- ences in preferences, attitudes, and certain difficult-to-define indi- vidual characteristics. It may be possible in the case of these variables to find subgroups of panel members with similar charac- teristics so that the influence of the first and second group of variables is revealed more clearly.

These considerations suggested to us that a simple model be set up appropriate to an evaluation of these kinds of variables. This simple model was then fitted to the observations of subgroups of the panel. It was apparent that the variance of two-year saving within each class was not constant but increased with income. We have, therefore, found that the data come closer to the homoscedastic re- quirement for efficient estimates of standard errors of the regression coefficients if we divide the saving variable by income. This treat- ment of the data also makes for better tests of the linearity of the saving relationships in our opinion.

The model which it is proposed to estimate may be written

$$(1) \left(\frac{s}{y}\right)_i = \alpha_0 + \alpha_1 x_{1i} + \alpha_2 x_{2i} + \ldots + \alpha_n x_{ni} + u_i$$

$$(i = 1, \ldots, 1059 \text{ spending units})$$

in which $\frac{s}{y}$ refers to the ratio of two-year saving to two-year income and the x_i represent explanatory variables to be defined shortly. The u refers to a random disturbance term. The subscript i runs over panel spending units. It is possible to test the linearity of the saving relationship by introducing two-year income among the explanatory variables. Significant coefficients associated with other variables may be interpreted as evidence that the marginal propensity to save shifts with the particular variable. The model is the simplest model which permits such inferences to be drawn.

The main idea of the model can be put in a negative fashion in this way: the rate of saving is hypothesized to be a constant unless the standard error of the regression coefficient is one-half or less of the coefficient itself. On a more positive note we may say that a significant coefficient indicates a linear shift in the marginal propen- sity to save with variation in the associated explanatory variable.

Ordinarily it is claimed that estimates of the regression coeffi- cients prepared from cross-section data are consistent and efficient, the former property being due to the independence of the explanatory variables and the disturbance term u. More specifically, it will be assumed that the random disturbance term u is distributed independently of the x variables and has a mean of zero and a finite variance. This assumption seems less tenable, however, in the case of our two-year measures of saving and income. One reason for this may be that spending units that plan to work more (multiple income earners) do so in order to save more, thus bringing about a degree of simultaneity in income and saving decisions which is not provided for in our model. A more delicate attack on this problem must be put aside for further research. Consequently, we do not make strong claims for our estimates which were obtained by single equation least squares methods.[1]

Measurement Considerations

For convenience' sake, we have assigned a symbol to each variable that may affect savings. In Table 5-1 these symbols are listed and the variables they represent are described briefly.

Our panel of 1059 consumer units is not a random sample of the population as a whole. Although the initial sample of consumers was picked by random selection methods, younger consumer units were not introduced into the panel in succeeding years and respondents who moved were not followed.[2] As a result, the members of our panel tend (1) to have higher incomes, (2) to contain a higher proportion of home owners, and (3) to be older than the noninstitutional population of the United States as a whole. Since it is not our aim to prepare estimates of aggregates but to estimate relationships, the randomness property of the sample is not considered vital. It is more important for our purposes to have an adequate range of variation of the variables of greatest interest to us. It will be of value to present some information on this last point which we shall do immediately after describing our procedure designed to measure saving (also see Appendix B).

---

[1]A more detailed discussion of some additional statistical and economic implications of a saving model that is similar but not identical to ours is given by Lawrence R. Klein and James N. Morgan, "Results of Alternative Statistical Treatment of Sample Survey Data," *Journal of the American Statistical Association*, XLVI, No. 256 (December 1951), 442-61.

[2]A multistage stratified probability sample of dwelling units was drawn for the first interview of the panel.

Table 5-1

VARIABLE INVENTORY

(All variables pertain to the spending unit)

Variable Symbol	Description	Measurement Field
S	Total saving rate during 1960 and 1961	Tenths of a per cent
S_d	Discretionary saving rate during 1960 and 1961	Tenths of a per cent
S_c	Contractual saving rate during 1960 and 1961	Tenths of a per cent
C_d	The rate of expenditures for major durables, cars, and housing repairs during 1960 and 1961	Tenths of a per cent
Y_2	Total money income during 1960 and 1961 divided by the number of people in the unit	Dollars per person
ΔY_2	Two-year change in income: 1961 total money income minus 1959 total money income	Dollars
L	Liquid asset holdings (checking and saving account balances and U.S. government bonds) early in 1960 divided by 1960 and 1961 total money income	Tenths of a per cent
$L\Delta Y$	Liquid asset holdings early in 1960 multiplied by the per cent income change 1960 to 1961	Dollars times a percentage
ΔL	Change in liquid asset holdings early 1959 to early 1960	Index values 0-9
P	Number of people in spending unit	Persons
A	Age of head of spending unit	Index values 0-9
E	Educational attainment of head	Index values 1-6
H	Housing status	Ownership = 1, nonownership = 0
Y_N	Normality of income situation during 1960 and 1961	Dummy variable
G	Receipt of gifts or inheritances	Dummy variable
Y_3	Income during 1959, 1960, and 1961 for the spending unit divided by 3	Dollars
Y_f	Anticipations of course of income over the next ten years	Dummy variable

Two-Year Saving Measure

To measure saving over two years, we asked respondents in the first interview early in 1960 about the dollar amounts of particular asset and debt items and asked again in the last interview early in 1962. Saving in each form was then calculated as the difference between two stock values. The components estimated in this way may be succinctly portrayed in an hypothetical consumer balance sheet in Table 5-2.

For a number of other saving components, respondents were asked early in 1961 and early in 1962 to report on the dollar amount of saving transactions during the prior years. These items, which are listed in Table 5-3, may be thought of as entering into the current account of consumers. Adding saving items measured by changes in balance sheet values to saving items measured by dollar amounts of saving transactions yielded the content of our saving measure.[3] Notice we are treating assets and debts in a symmetrical way but with opposite signs. Not included in saving are accumulations in the form of currency, pension reserves, social security reserves, durable consumer goods, or changes in asset value due to depreciation or capital gains or losses. With respect to one asset item in particular we asked the respondent to distinguish between net accumulations of common stocks and changes in holdings due to capital gains or losses. Only the first value was included in our concept of saving.[4] Consequently, we shall not be able to study the influence of capital gains and losses upon saving behavior.

An interesting question for purposes of subsequent analysis is:

---

[3]We are likely to be mingling different kinds of errors including response errors by these practices. These problems deserve more attention than we have yet been able to give them. A discussion of methods of validating response errors and a presentation of results of a substantive study are contained in John B. Lansing, G. P. Ginsburg, and Kaisa Braaten, *An Investigation of Response Error* (Urbana, Illinois: University of Illinois, 1961), especially pp. 118-53. A discussion of the possibility of adjusting the data is contained in Irwin Friend and Stanley Schor, "Who Saves?" *Review of Economics and Statistics,* LXI, No. 2 (May 1959), Part I.

[4]The question asked early in 1962 was: "Stock prices change and people put money into stocks and take money out. Did you put new money into stock or take money out 'on balance' over the last two years?" "How much?$____."

Table 5-2

CONSUMER BALANCE SHEET

Assets	Liabilities
Liquid assets:	Personal debt
Checking and savings accounts	Installment debt
U.S. government savings bonds	Other personal nonmedical debt
Various other assets:	
	Debt on real property
Bonds	
	Owner-occupied house
U.S. government other than savings	Farm
State and local government	Other
Corporate	
Mortgages and land contracts	
Real property other than houses lived in (business and farm equipment)	

Table 5-3

SAVINGS ITEMS IN CURRENT ACCOUNT
TRANSACTIONS

Expenditures (added)	Receipts (subtracted)
Life insurance premiums[a]	Inheritances and gifts
Mortgage principal repayments	Sales of securities
Additions to owner-occupied houses	
Purchases of securities (net additions to holdings)	
Net profit left in business or farm	

[a]No attempt was made to separate the saving component from the insurance component.

who engages in what kind of saving transactions? The data presented in Table 5-4 provide some preliminary answers.

1. Most of the panel members engaged in *contractual saving transactions* (insurance premium payments and repayment of residential mortgages), although the proportion does vary markedly with income.

2. *Liquid asset transactions* as we have defined them were engaged in by the largest proportion of panel members. However, again the proportion varies appreciably with income.

3. Less than half the panel engaged in transactions involving *stocks or bonds* and those panel members that did engage in such transactions were concentrated in the upper income groups.

4. Relatively few members of the panel engage in *business or farm transactions* and these units are concentrated in the higher income classes. This finding indicates that it would be useful to study the self-employed group separately. To the extent that nonmoney income is important to farmers, we have a good reason to put off any systematic study of the farm subsample because we did not attempt to measure nonmoney income.

An interesting concentration of debt transactions is to be observed in the group with an average 1960 and 1961 income between $4000 and $15,000. The proportion of panel members who engaged in such transactions declined in the lower and higher income classes. These patterns may alert the research worker to expect nonlinear relationships between saving and income.

Several other features of the measurement of saving are noteworthy. Available for experimentation will be a comparatively comprehensive measure which comes close to an estimate of the change in consumer net worth although accumulations of durable goods inventories were not included. The usefulness of our measurement practices depend on how close we have come to what consumers have in mind when they think of saving, a concept which may vary among groups. Our measure of saving is not satisfactory from the viewpoint of employment analysis as it includes elements which stimulate employment (e.g., accumulation of new housing equity) as well as

Table 5-4

PER CENT OF ALL PANEL SPENDING UNITS REPORTING SELECTED ASSET
OR DEBT TRANSACTIONS

Average 1960-1961 income	Per cent of sample	Type of asset or debt item					
		Contractual assets saving (insurance premiums and repayment of residential mortgages)	Liquid assets	Miscellaneous investments (purchase or sale of stock or bonds)	Business or farm assets	Additions to houses	Consumer debt
Under $1000	4	42	44	*	*	*	24
$1000-1999	9	45	60	*	*	20	34
$2000-2999	9	68	74	19	*	30	53
$3000-3999	8	68	77	16	*	20	56
$4000-4999	11	80	84	*	12	30	64
$5000-5999	10	92	96	*	*	30	69
$6000-7499	15	92	93	28	*	41	71
$7500-9999	15	99	97	32	13	49	78
$10,000-14,999	11	97	98	55	22	58	66
$15,000 or more	5	100	98	53	38	62	49
Income not available	3						

*Less than one-half of one per cent.

elements which do not stimulate employment (e.g., accumulation of liquid assets).

A distinction was drawn between discretionary and contractual saving by excluding from the former category insurance premium payments and mortgage principle repayments. It was assumed that these were the consequences of saving decisions made prior to the two-year period. All other items including changes in debt are included in the discretionary component. As a result of this distinction three separate saving variables were prepared: a discretionary, a contractual, and a total saving income ratio. The contractual saving income ratio is considered to be an independent variable in the analysis on the grounds that the decisions to purchase insurance or to incur a mortgage were made prior to the two-year period of interest of us. Preparation of the contractual saving income ratio as a variable enables us to test a number of ideas such as whether or not contractual and discretionary saving, as we have defined them, are substitutes for each other.[5]

In the traditional view of consumer behavior it is often asserted that the rate of saving is determined, although with some degree of uncertainty, by a process of rational choice which depends on the preferences of the individual[6] and certain outside facts. Among these "outside facts" are the consumer's income and wealth. We turn to a tabular presentation of the relation among these key variables.

What impressions can be gained from a conditional distribution of the total saving rate within two-year income classes? It may be noted that the marginal distribution of the total saving rate is skewed off to the positive values (Table 5-5). The conditional distribution of the total saving rate exhibits an interesting feature when controlled by income class: the proportion of extreme values both positive and negative tends to increase with income suggesting that our effort to achieve homoscedasticity of the dependent variable with respect to income was not completely successful. It appears also from scanning the table that the saving rate shifts with income although it is not a

---

[5]There is some evidence that they are not close substitutes. This matter was explored by William C. Reher in an unpublished Ph.D. thesis: "A Cross-Section Analysis of Contractual Saving," University of Michigan, 1957.

[6]Trygve Haavelmo, "Econometric Analysis of the Savings Survey Data," *Bulletin of the Oxford University Institute of Statistics,* Vol. 19, No. 2 (May 1957), p. 146.

Table 5-5

TWO-YEAR SAVING RATE BY AVERAGE TWO-YEAR INCOME

(Percentage distribution of 1059 panel members)

Total two-year saving as a per cent of two-year income	All cases	Average total money income of the spending unit for 1960 and 1961										Not ascertained
		Under $1000	$1000-1999	$2000-2999	$3000-3999	$4000-4999	$5000-5999	$6000-7499	$7500-9999	$10,000-14,999	$15,000 or more	
Plus 50 or more	7	3	12	8	7	4	5	5	6	12	9	6
Plus 30-49	6	2	2	6	9	9	7	5	6	7	13	0
Plus 20-29	10	5	6	4	8	9	11	13	12	12	11	15
Plus 10-19	19	5	10	10	14	14	20	27	31	21	19	6
Plus 1-9	26	24	19	29	30	31	23	28	25	27	13	22
Zero (no saving)	3	29	14	0	3	1	0	0	0	0	0	18
Minus 1-9	9	2	13	12	6	11	15	11	9	4	6	6
Minus 10-24	7	5	9	14	8	8	7	5	5	5	4	9
Minus 25 or less	7	22	9	11	7	8	7	3	2	2	6	6
Not ascertained	6	3	6	6	8	5	5	3	4	10	19	12
Total	100	100	100	100	100	100	100	100	100	100	100	100
Per cent of sample	100	4	9	9	8	11	10	15	15	11	5	3

sharp shift. Whether such a relationship will persist after a more multivariate analysis remains to be seen.

A conditional distribution of the total saving rate by amount of liquid assets held at the beginning of the period (early 1960) is made available in Table 5-6. About four out of five panel members reported nonzero amounts and almost one-third reported amounts of $2000. This variation in liquid asset holdings will help in providing a more interesting test of the influence of this variable upon saving. It is quite difficult, however, to observe any systematic variation with assets but it is quite easy to observe the increased variation of the dependent variable as liquid asset holdings increase. The proportion of both high and low saving rates increases with these assets. At first glance this spread suggests that a disaggregation among groups in the sample in different saving situations ought to be rewarding.[7]

Alerted by a suggestion of T. C. Koopmans as to the possible distorting effects of gifts and inheritances upon estimated saving relationships, we took steps to remove these items from our concept of saving and to distinguish from other spending units those that had received gifts and inheritances.[8] An illustration may be given which indicates how gifts and inheritances may distort estimates of saving relations. Suppose the measure of wealth did not distinguish between gifts and inheritances and other components. Suppose further that consumers who have received gifts and inheritances are concentrated in the group reporting large liquid asset holdings. If gifts and inheritances do not influence saving in the same way that accumulations of liquid assets out of income do, then the estimated relation between liquid assets and saving will be distorted by the inclusion of observations from consumers with gifts and inheritances. For example, if liquid assets accumulated out of income press downward on the saving rate but gifts and inheritances do not, then consumers with gifts and inheritances among their liquid assets will report higher than expected saving rates. It is assumed that we do not know which

---

[7]A consideration of reasons underlying the varied saving characteristics of high asset consumers is presented in George Katona, "On the So-called Wealth Effect," *Review of Economics and Statistics,* XLIII (February, 1961). Tables presenting finer classifications (from the same panel) are made available in an article by Charles A. Lininger, "Estimates of Rates of Saving," *Journal of Political Economy,* LXXII, No. 3 (June 1964), 306-11.

[8]T. C. Koopmans, *Three Essays on the State of Economic Science* (New York: McGraw-Hill Book Co., 1957), p. 207.

Table 5-6

TWO-YEAR SAVING RATE BY AMOUNT OF LIQUID ASSETS

(Percentage distribution of 1059 panel members)

Total two-year saving as a per cent of two-year income	All cases	Total liquid assets, January-February 1960								
		None	$1-99	$100-199	$200-499	$500-999	$1000-1999	$2000-4999	$5000-9999	$10,000 or more
Plus 50 or more	7	3	2	4	7	4	6	8	11	26
Plus 30-49	6	3	3	9	7	9	5	9	9	2
Plus 20-29	10	9	11	7	11	11	13	9	9	9
Plus 10-19	19	18	17	23	27	21	20	17	15	7
Plus 1-9	26	34	39	32	24	25	28	19	12	12
Zero (no saving)	3	17	0	0	0	0	1	1	1	0
Minus 1-9	9	7	10	15	10	11	8	10	4	12
Minus 10-24	7	3	11	4	4	9	7	11	9	4
Minus 25 or less	7	0	1	2	4	4	6	9	20	25
Not ascertained	6	6	6	4	6	6	6	7	10	3
Total	100	100	100	100	100	100	100	100	100	100
Per cent of sample	100	17	9	7	12	13	13	15	8	6

consumers have received gifts and inheritances. This illustration may explain the high saving rates of large asset holders observable in Table 5-6. We shall find out later that this is not the explanation of the high saving rates, but it is a plausible one that we felt ought to be investigated.

Two-year Income Measure

The income variable used in this study is an estimate of total money income available to the consumer unit during 1960 and 1961—the two-year period over which savings were measured. The questionnaire was designed to obtain information on money incomes received from both market and nonmarket sources (the income section of the questionnaire is reproduced in Appendix A). The respondent was asked about specific sources of income such as professional practice, dividends, and unemployment compensation benefits. Information on income from all income earners in the consumer unit was also obtained. (Our first preference would have been to prepare a measure of income after taxes but this would have required estimating deductions and exemptions.)

For a number of reasons it was decided to divide this income measure by the number of people in the consumer unit. It was assumed that, other things equal, a family with more members is likely to save less than a family with fewer members. Calculating per member income is only one way of allowing for the influence of family size, however. It has been suggested by several readers that it would have been preferable to divide total income by the number of equivalent adults so as to avoid treating the very young as having the same weight upon saving decisions as the teenager, or the college age member.[9] This clearly is a desirable step when resources permit such treatment.

The question of the appropriate consumer wealth variable to use in the saving relationships has a number of theoretical and measurement aspects. It can be argued that the wealth variable ought to be the stock counterpart of the saving flows. Unfortunately, for our purposes some of the saving components were estimated directly as

[9] Professors Robin Barlow and Wilbur Thompson provided helpful comments on this point.

flows so that information on initial stocks was not available. It was decided to use initial liquid assets as a wealth variable. To the extent consumers maintain a constant share of total wealth in the form of liquid assets, changes in liquid assets may be a decent proxy for wealth changes.[10]   Liquid asset holdings were divided by two-year income.

Several specially constructed variables may be dealt with at this point. Other variables will be taken up in the course of the discussion of the results. One variable permitted us to examine interactions between liquid assets and income change. Another enabled us to sort panel members into groups according to whether or not during 1960 and 1961 they appeared to us to be on their trend income position, or above, or below it. With respect to the income change-liquid asset interaction variable, we multiplied the two-year income change over 1960 and 1961 by initial liquid assets. A negative income change together with nonzero asset holdings could be associated in this way with a lower or negative saving rate. The influence of a negative income change together with no liquid asset holdings upon the saving rate was dampened by assigning zero to all such cases.

It seemed advantageous to distinguish groups in typical or normal income situations from others. It was done in a straightforward way: a comparison was made of the reported changes in income from 1959 to 1960 and from 1960 to 1961 to the anticipated income change from 1961 to 1962. If the changes were of the same sign, the spending unit was classified as being in a normal situation. If the signs were reversed, the income situation of the spending unit was classified as being abnormal. Fluctuating incomes were also distinguished. An explicit account of the preparation of this variable is presented in the appendix to this chapter.[11]

[10]A critical view is taken by Franco Modigliani and Albert K. Ando, "Tests of the Life Cycle Hypothesis of Savings," *Bulletin of the Oxford University Institute of Statistics,* Vol. 19, No. 2 (May 1957), p. 118. However, there are data to support the view that the proportion of liquid assets to total assets within wide ranges is relatively constant: George Katona and John B. Lansing, "The Wealth of the Wealthy," *The Review of Economics and Statistics,* XLVI (February 1, 1964), Table 5, p. 7.

[11]In preparation of this variable, we followed a suggestion of Professor Jean Crockett in "Income and Asset Effects on Consumption: Aggregate and Cross Section," *Models of Income Determination, Studies in Income and Wealth,* XXVIII (Princeton: National Bureau of Economic Research, 1951), 223.

Estimated Saving Relationships for the Entire Panel

What results may be obtained from estimating the parameters of the basic model from the data reported by all panel members? These initial results are desired as bench marks against which the additional insight to be obtained from disaggregation may be measured.

Total Saving Rate

A straightforward model in which the total saving rate was made to depend upon income, prior build-up in liquid assets, and simple demographic variables was estimated with the following consequences (equation 1):[12]

1. (921 panel members).[13]

$$S = 1.004 + .0006 \ Y_2 + .298 \ \Delta L + 1.215 \ P + .684 \ A.$$
$$(1.276) \ (.0003) \qquad (.494) \qquad (.866) \quad (1.052) \qquad R = .08$$

The coefficient of the income variable, Y_2, is positive and significant, consistent with the view that the relationship between total saving and two year income is nonlinear. This finding is in a general way the same as the evidence of curvature obtained when saving equations are fitted to one-year measures of savings and income. At an average annual income during 1960 and 1961 of $7000, the estimated marginal propensity to save out of two-year income may be calculated to be about .09. It will be remembered, when considering the correlation coefficient of .08, that total saving have been divided by income so that it is variation in the saving rate that makes up the dependent variable.

With respect to the change in liquid assets 1959 to 1960, it was not clear a priori what a build-up in liquid assets would imply for the total saving rate. Such a build-up might for example, be associated with an existing preference for saving or conversely such a build-up might lead to an increased preference for saving. In either case a positive coefficient might be expected. On the other hand, a negative

---

[12]In the calculations presented in this chapter, classical least squares methods were utilized to obtain parameter estimates. The figures in parentheses below the regression coefficients are standard errors.

[13]Only panel members reporting information on all the variables were included.

coefficient might be expected if one accepts this model as relevant to a test of a saturation or Pigou effect.[14] The coefficient is positive in this instance but the standard error easily covers zero so that we are unable to offer, at this point, good evidence in support of any one of these views. Although the spending unit size variable might be expected to exert a negative influence upon the saving rate, the coefficient is positive. The standard error is so large that little can be said about this result with confidence. The coefficient associated with age is positive as expected but hardly significant.

Discretionary Saving Rate

The discretionary saving rate as a component of the total saving rate ought to be subject to shorter run phenomena than the contractual saving rate. A slightly different specification was, therefore, attempted. The two-year change in income was included among the explanatory variables. Initial liquid assets as a stock rather than rate of change variable was introduced with the following results:

2. (746 panel members).

$$S_d = 7.470 + .0002\ Y_2 + .135\ \Delta Y_2 + .028\ L + .560\ P \qquad R = .10$$
$$\quad (1.124)\ (.0003)\quad (.057)\qquad (.018)\qquad (.873)$$

The idea of the constancy of the discretionary saving rate (7.47 per cent) with respect to two-year income cannot be rejected in view of the size of the standard error of the regression coefficient associated with income. There is no evidence of curvature here. Highly significant is the coefficient associated with the variable measuring the two-year change in income which reveals a positive association between income change and the saving rate. This variable was measured as a roughly scaled index so that the magnitude of the coefficient cannot be interpreted as more than an indicator of the direction of influence. In Chapter 3 an intensive effort was made to analyze the income change variable into simpler events, but we are not able to introduce these finer gradations into the equation at present. Of considerable interest is the positive sign of the coefficient associated

---

[14] These possibilities have been described at greater length by George Katona in *The Powerful Consumer* (New York: McGraw-Hill, 1960), p. 136.

with initial liquid asset holdings. We have already noted the argument that an increase in wealth, other things being equal, tends to reduce the proportion saved out of a given income. This hypothetical wealth effect does not appear to be operating in the assumed direction, although assertions at this stage cannot be made with much confidence because, for one thing, the standard error is quite large.

Estimated Saving Relationships
for Subgroups of the Panel

These initial preliminary efforts to estimate saving relationships for the entire panel have not yielded results which can be discussed with much confidence. It is apparent that to make progress some complications will have to be introduced. Our choice is to distinguish subgroups of the sample using both objective and subjective type variables to accomplish this purpose.

Employee Spending Units

The first major disaggregation we made in investigating the saving relationship of subgroups of the panel was to distinguish employees and the self-employed. This subdivision was chosen for two reasons:

1. One of the most widely reported empirical results of saving studies has been the finding that the saving function of consumer units headed by self-employed people has a higher slope than the schedule of other groups.[15]

2. The sample size for the self-employed was quite small (66), too small for any serious inquiry into the financial affairs of this group (which tend to be complicated).

It was decided at the same time to separate out units with heads who were retired and study them separately also. However, our main efforts will be concentrated upon the employee group.

Consequently, it may be asked whether new information is made

---

[15]Results are reported, for example, by L. R. Klein in *Contributions of Survey Methods to Economics* (New York: Columbia University Press, 1954), p. 228ff.

available if equations are fitted to observations obtained from a sub-sample of spending units headed by people who are employed by others. Several similarities and several rather striking differences between equation 2 for the panel and equation 3 for the subgroup are apparent:

3. (645 employee panel members).

$$S_d = -.543 + .0000\ Y_2 + .061\ \Delta Y_2 - .104\ L + 1.281\ A.$$
$$(.682)\ (.0002)\quad\ (.045)\quad\ \ (.019)\quad\ \ (.671)\qquad R = .22$$

In neither equation do we find evidence of curvature with respect to income for the discretionary saving rate. We do find a difference in the lack of significance of the coefficient associated with the two-year change of income for the subgroup although the sign remains positive. Consequently, the conclusion may be drawn that a two-year change in income is positively associated with two-year saving for one of the excluded groups (the self-employed in fact) and not significantly associated with two-year saving among the employee subgroup. Two-year change in income may tend more frequently to be changes in the trend of income compared, say, to one-year income changes. It is of interest, therefore, to find this difference in saving behavior between the self-employed and others. It is as if the self-employed view these changes in income, if positive, as opportunities to accumulate wealth at a yet higher rate.

A striking difference is to be observed in the sign and significance of the coefficient associated with initial liquid asset holdings (as a per cent of two-year income). The coefficient becomes negative and highly significant indicative of a quite different influence upon the discretionary saving rate among this subgroup than among the excluded groups. Previous saving studies have indicated that the influence of liquid assets upon saving behavior depends upon the income level of the consumer.[16] It will be worthwhile to probe more deeply into this result in order to see whether it is observable in the case of the two-year saving rate. With the variable at our disposal it will be possible to test whether this result is due to some error of measurement.

---

[16]An early discussion is contained in L. R. Klein in "Assets, Debts, and Economic Behavior," *Studies in Income & Wealth,* XIV. (New York: National Bureau of Economic Research, 1951), 223.

Before pursuing the subject of liquid assets it will be valuable to exploit panel data in another direction. It may be argued that the consumer's saving decisions are influenced by the level of income over a longer period than two years. As a step in this direction we introduce an average of income over three years.[17] What this variable introduces that is new into the model is income in 1959 or the income of the year prior to the two-year saving period. This variable supposes that the prior period's income together with the current income is of some consequence in saving behavior.

4. (653 employee panel members).

$$S_d = -.367 + .0004 \ Y_3 - .105 \ L + .341 \ P + .905 \ A.$$
$$(.678) \ (.0002) \quad (.019) \quad (.399) \quad (.626)$$

$$R = .23$$

The first result of interest is that the coefficient associated with three-year average income is positive and significant at the conventional level. Thus, three-year income appears to exert a significant influence upon the discretionary saving rate, whereas a measure of two-year income does not. This may mean that the level of the prior year's income was of importance in determining the current saving rate because of some lag or period of adjustment in the consumer's saving behavior. That is, high levels of income in 1959 may have been associated with a high rate of spending which was followed by a high rate of saving. This line of reasoning is quite speculative.

The coefficient associated with initial liquid assets is highly significant and negative and very little changed in value from the results obtained in equation 3. Neither size of spending unit nor age of head can be said to exhibit a significant influence in this model.

To return to the issues of the role of liquid assets or wealth in saving behavior, it is now appropriate to undertake a systematic exploration of this phenomenon. In the approach chosen, the same saving model is fitted to observations from various subgroups in the panel. The equations are presented in the columns of Table 5-7. The most striking result is the change in sign of the liquid asset variable from subgroup to subgroup.

---

[17]A critic may well note that we have changed our maintained hypothesis from equation to equation so that we can no longer make exact probability statements. We choose a pragmatic point of view at this stage because of the small amount of a priori information available on the role of many variables which would appear, plausibly, to enter into saving behavior.

Table 5-7

REGRESSION COEFFICIENTS FOR TWO-YEAR DISCRETIONARY SAVING-INCOME RATE EQUATIONS

(For selected groups of employee spending units)

Variable definitions	Employee Spending Unit Groups							
	Classified by income		Classified by receipt of gifts or inheritances				Classified by income anticipations	
	Two-year average income less than $7500	Two-year average income $7500 or more	Two-year average income less than $7500; no gifts or inheritances	Two-year average income less than $7500 received gifts or inheritances	Two-year average income $7500 or more; no gifts or inheritances	Two-year average income $7500 or more; received gifts inheritances	Two-year average income less than $7500; anticipated income trend up	Two-year average income more than $7500; anticipated income trend up
Equation number	5	6	7	8	9	10	11	12
Constant term	.617 (.934)	6.904 (1.254)	5.692 (.823)	-19.183 (4.774)	8.419 (1.195)	27.562 (3.087)	6.169 (1.463)	13.653 (1.809)
Two-year income divided by spending unit size	.0000 (.0003)	-.0002 (.0002)	-.0006 (.0007)	.0008 (.0018)	-.0003 (.0003)	-.0006 (.0007)	-.0007 (.0007)	.0006 (.0003)
Liquid assets held early in 1960 divided by two-year income	-.071 (.021)	.101 (.089)	-.111 (.019)	-.164 (.163)	.084 (.080)	.307 (.310)	-.243 (.058)	.290 (.105)
Change in liquid assets from early 1959 to early 1960	-.419 (.419)	.205 (.419)						
Size of spending unit in early 1962			-1.217 (.611)	3.904 (4.389)	-.871 (1.012)	-1.586 (3.426)	-.707 (1.168)	.729 (1.379)
Age of head of spending unit as of early 1962	.991 (.776)	-.482 (1.439)	1.136 (.685)	1.319 (4.839)	.426 (1.406)	-3.645 (3.758)	1.495 (1.309)	-4.207 (2.161)
Correlation coefficient*	.21	.12	.32	.31	.12	.22	.27	.24
Number of spending units in group	316	203	370	33	206	44	268	218

*Not adjusted for degrees of freedom.

Consider first equation 5 and 6 in which the subgroup of employee headed consumer units is further subdivided into two groups: those units receiving an average of $7500 or more during the period 1960 and 1961 and those receiving less than that amount. This amount was chosen more or less arbitrarily based, however, on an intuitive notion of a minimum income which permits some discretionary decisions.[18] It will be noted that the hypothesis that the saving rate is constant, independent of the influence of income cannot be rejected in either equation 5 or 6. It may be said that the constant rate of about 7 per cent in the case of higher income consumer units differs significantly from zero while the intercept in the case of the lower income units cannot be said to differ from zero.

The sign of the coefficient associated with liquid assets changes from negative in the case of low income families to positive in the case of high income families, although the coefficient cannot be taken to be significantly different from zero in the latter case. This striking contrast, similar to results obtained with saving and income measured over one year, suggests that a rather different interpretation of the role of wealth as a stock variable—as reflected in liquid assets—may usefully be constructed for high and low income groups.

The difference in sign associated with liquid assets remains after exclusion of the group receiving gifts and inheritances (equations 7 through 10). If anything, the negative influence of liquid assets is brought out even more sharply among the group of low income consumer units who did not receive gifts and inheritances. Consequently, we believe we have answered the possible criticism that our results are due to the distorting influence of gifts and inheritances in our measure of wealth. The positive sign remains for both high income groups, those who did and those who did not receive gifts and inheritances. The standard errors are extremely large in these last two equations and easily cover zero. There does not appear to be any evidence that there is any marked difference in saving behavior between the last two groups; i.e., between high income consumers distinguished by the receipt of gifts and inheritances.

Having disaggregated by an objective-type variable such as the

[18]It is left to future research to determine in a more experimental manner the dividing point between low and high incomes. This point becomes very important when we consider the influence of liquid assets upon the saving rate in more aggregative models.

reported receipt of gifts and inheritances, we turn to a subjective or anticipatory variable available from the panel interviews. It may be asked whether saving behavior differs according to whether the respondent is optimistic or pessimistic about future income. Consider in equations 11 and 12 the low and high income groups which reported optimistic future income prospects. According to one widely accepted interpretation these groups ought to tend to save less than others because they anticipate rising income prospects and may be thought, currently, to be below their normal income level. What in fact do we find? In both cases we find that the intercepts are higher than the intercepts for the equations for all low and high income units. In the case of the low income units, the intercept is significantly different from zero although the income effect is nonsignificant. However, there is no evidence that the optimistic low income group save less than the others. In the case of high income units, the evidence is even more striking that these optimistic units save more. The intercept is higher than the intercept of other groups, the slope income coefficient is positive and highly significant, and the shift coefficient associated with liquid assets is positive and highly significant. Consequently the high income, high asset, and optimistic group appear to be the highest savers among our employee group. It may be that concrete and attainable rewards stimulate saving.[19]

Having made these comments about the role of liquid assets in the saving relationship, we find a great many questions yet to be discussed. If some respondents with average incomes under $7500 were only temporarily in this income bracket (experiencing temporary income declines), the negative coefficient could be interpreted as evidence of dissaving in these circumstances. For this reason, and others, it seemed advantageous to distinguish groups in typical or normal situations from others, leaving the definition of the situation to the respondent as much as possible. Mention has been made already of this variable and a fuller account is given in the appendix to this chapter. The results are available in Table 5-8.

The reversal in the sign associated with initial liquid asset

---

[19]See, for example, George Katona, *The Powerful Consumer, op. cit.,* p. 107. I am also indebted to Professor Walter Williams for calling my attention to this point which is discussed in an unpublished paper of his, "Inadequacies in the Determination of the Value of Pension Promises and Their Possible Effect Upon Studies of Consumer Behavior."

Table 5-8

REGRESSION COEFFICIENTS FOR TWO-YEAR DISCRETIONARY SAVING RATE EQUATIONS
FOR GROUPS DEFINED BY REPORTED AND ANTICIPATED INCOMES

(For 712 employee spending units)

Variable definitions	Spending units expecting a continuation of income trend, average 1960 and 1961 income over $7500	Spending units expecting a continuation of income trend, average 1960 and 1961 income under $7500	Spending units expecting a decreased income reversing the trend	Spending units expecting an increased income reversing the trend	Spending units expecting a continuation of fluctuating incomes
Equation number	13	14	15	16	17
Constant term	4.868 (1.500)	.386 (1.200)	-17.375 (1.550)	-1.748 (1.700)	-1.341 (1.650)
Size of spending unit	-2.100 (1.336)	-.528 (.801)	1.118 (1.333)	.415 (1.255)	-1.798 (1.755)
Age of head	1.412 (1.752)	.124 (.973)	1.837 (1.707)	-.251 (1.693)	.634 (2.084)
Educational attainment of head	.362 (1.118)	-.765 (.922)	.896 (1.138)	-1.327 (1.500)	-.814 (1.802)
Size of place	.978 (1.003)	.573 (.652)	.324 (1.138)	.325 (.962)	2.148 (1.505)
Change in liquid assets from early 1959 to early 1960	-.118 (.470)	-.135 (.441)	1.574 (.604)	.727 (.589)	-.430 (.811)
Housing status	5.827 (4.330)	4.609 (2.364)	2.551 (4.262)	4.153 (3.669)	5.722 (5.696)
Contractual saving income ratio	-.229 (.200)	.029 (.108)	.204 (.175)	-.029 (.305)	.144 (.328)
Liquid asset income ratio early 1960	.159 (.100)	-.254 (.041)	-.400 (.073)	-.076 (.015)	.194 (.216)
Two-year income divided by spending unit size	.007 (.004)	.005 (.005)	.006 (.004)	.004 (.006)	.004 (.014)
Correlation coefficient[a]	.30	.39	.58	.57	.45
Number of spending units	161	263	103	104	44

[a]Not adjusted for loss of degrees of freedom.

holdings between high and for low income units remains for both groups of spending units in "normal income" situations (equations 13 and 14). For those spending units apparently enjoying temporarily high incomes (equation 15), large initial asset holdings depressed the saving rate considerably—a result of considerable interest. It is as if unusually high incomes combined with large liquid asset holdings resulted in an upward shift in the spending rate. The coefficients of equation 16 suggest that unusually low incomes combined with large liquid assets resulted in a modest reduction in the saving rate, that is, liquid asset holdings did depress the saving rate in these circumstances.[20] For those spending units reporting fluctuating incomes, the influence of liquid assets upon the saving rate appears to be negligible although it is of some interest that the sign becomes positive.

It may be noted that little, if any, evidence of curvature of the saving relationship with respect to income is apparent in Table 5.8. Nor can much support be obtained for many plausible hypotheses with respect to the influence of other economic and social variables upon the saving rate. What remains is a sensitivity of the saving rate to initial liquid asset holdings. It will be noted that disaggregation by normality of income situation has led to relatively high correlation coefficients.

Estimated Saving Relationships for the Self-Employed and the Retired

In turning to the self-employed subgroup, we must restrain our research efforts because of the limitations of small sample size and scant information on complicated financial affairs. We can, however, fit a few equations to the data for purposes of comparison. Consider in equation 18 a very simple model designed to test for the nonlinear effects of income.

---

[20] These results are similar to the results of an earlier study in which one-year savings were found to decline under the influence of temporary income decreases. George Katona, "The Effect of Income Changes on the Rate of Saving," *Review of Economics and Statistics*, XXXI, No. 2 (May 1949), 103.

18. (66 self-employed panel members)

$$S_d = .797 + .0014 \ Y_2 + 3.657 \ P - 3.079 \ A.$$
$$(5.365) \ (.0007) \quad (4.825) \quad (6.318)$$

R = .32.

For self-employed spending units, evidence of a nonlinear saving relationship is available in the significant coefficient associated with two-year income. This result is consistent with the results of many other quantitative studies of the saving behavior of self-employed or entrepreneurial households carried out with one-year measures of saving and income.[21]

It may be of interest to inquire about the influence of changes in income measured over two years, such changes very likely, as we have remarked, representing trends in income rather than temporary fluctuations. Consider equation 19:

19. (47 self-employed panel members)

$$S_d = 37.583 + .0010 \ Y_2 - 8.006 \ A + .0083 \ L \ \Delta Y + 3.091 \ L.$$
$$(6.402) \ (.0007) \quad (6.093) \quad (.0036) \quad (2.942)$$

R = .47.

in which the rate of change of income over two years is multiplied by liquid assets in order to provide an interaction variable which permits dissaving if nonzero assets are held. The positive significant coefficient indicates the willingness of the self-employed to dissave if assets permit (for business purposes?) as well as the willingness to save at a higher rate when income increases are experienced. These results are similar to results achieved with one-year measures.[22]

In the case of spending units headed by a retired person, it will be noted that there is no evidence of a shift in the marginal propensity to save as two-year income varies. The difference in saving behavior between the self-employed and the retired indicates once again the importance of being able to disaggregate the total cross-section sample into more homogeneous subgroups. Consider equation 20:

---

[21] For example, Malcolm R. Fisher, "Explorations in Saving Behavior," *Bulletin of the Oxford University Institute of Statistics*, Vol. 18, No. 3 (August 1956), Table 2.1, p. 232.

[22] L. R. Klein, "The British Propensity to Save," *Journal of the Royal Statistical Society*, Vol. 121 (1958), p. 67.

20. (122 retired panel members).

$$S_d = 15.606 + .0001\ Y_2 + .0047\ L\Delta Y + 3.929\ P - 3.080\ D.$$
$$\quad\quad (5.203)\ (.0019) \quad\ (.0010) \quad\quad (5.177) \quad (2.814)$$

$$R = .39.$$

The coefficient of the income change liquid asset interaction variable supports the view that retired people who have assets to begin with want to maintain consumption levels when confronted with income declines. D, the rate of expenditures on durable goods, appears to be inversely related to discretionary savings, but the standard error is large. Both groups, self-employed and retired, deserve more intensive study than we are able to give them at this time.

Summary

In a negative way these studies of the two-year saving rate suggest that additional research which aims for results by aggregating the dependent variable over time, say, over two, three or more years ought to proceed with caution. Little encouragement can be supplied such efforts on the basis of the results of our studies. On the contrary, it would appear that something has been lost in such aggregation over time. We believe that the dynamics of consumer saving behavior can be more usefully explored in terms of variables measured over a year or perhaps less. Further research is called for which attempts to find out what time span appears to be in the consumers' mind when he undertakes saving transactions. It is possible that the time span will differ depending upon such considerations as the education and occupation of the employed members of the consumer unit or the life cycle stage of the unit. Further work in this direction with the panel data at our disposal may prove valuable in this connection although it could not be undertaken at the present time.

In a more positive vein we can report that there is evidence of a nonlinear marginal propensity to save out of two-year income when equations are fitted to observations from the entire panel. This result is largely due to the presence of the self-employed in the panel, but also partly due to optimistic high income consumers, another interesting subgroup.

One of the most intriguing results of the present study is the finding that the role of initial liquid assets in the saving behavior of high income and low income consumers seems to be quite different. Several steps forward in exploring this phenomenon may be claimed. That this result could be spurious due to the inclusion of consumers who had received gifts or inheritances is an anxiety that can now be relaxed. That this result could be spurious due to consumers being in unusual income situations is an argument that is not consistent with the results we have obtained from consumers in "normal" income situations (as we have defined a normal income situation). Among low income spending units a Pigou type or depressing effect of liquid assets upon the saving rate is observable, but it seems to be quite unlike the effect envisioned in this theory. The positive influence of liquid assets upon the saving rate of high income consumers requires, it seems to us, additional research effort.[23]

We have been able to explain a somewhat larger part of the variation of the saving rate than we had expected (see Table 5-8), but much remains to be done in the way of specifying more delicate forms of the saving relation and in specifying additional variables likely to enter the saving relation. We have not touched the question of the influence of pension plan provisions upon the saving rate, a question about which research is now underway.

---

[23]Among the questions deserving study is the following one: Will our results be observable if a more comprehensive measure of wealth is introduced into the saving relation? A spectrum of wealth measures could be constructed from the panel data ranging from demand deposits to a measure rather close to net worth. Further research along these lines is projected.

Appendix To Chapter 5

Definitions of Specially Constructed
Variables

1. A variable indicating whether or not family assets or reserves were composed of gifts or inheritances was constructed from answers to the question in the 1961 Survey of Consumer Finances.

"Considering your total family assets or reserve funds now—did most of them come from inheritances or gifts, or did you save most of them out of income?"

The answers were coded:

1. All from inheritance or gifts; inheritance
2. Most from inheritance, but not all
3. 50 per cent; about half; some from each
4. Mostly out of income, but not all
5. All from income; income
7. Inherited or received gift, etc., but no longer any reserves
9. Don't know, not ascertained

0. Inappropriate; no reserves.

Codes 1, 2, and 3 defined spending units with inheritances of gifts for purposes of this study.

2. A variable indicating future long-run income anticipations was prepared from answers to the following question asked in the 1961 Survey of Consumer Finances:

"During the next ten years or so, do you think your earnings will rise gradually, go up and down from year to year, or fall or what?"

1. Rise gradually; rises
2. Stay the same; about the same

3. Fall gradually; fall (including "will retire")
7. Go up and down from year to year, fluctuate a lot
9. Don't know, not ascertained
0. Inappropriate; head is retired or a housewife

3. Panel groups in different income situations defined with respect to reported income changes 1959 to 1960 and 1960 to 1961 and anticipated income change 1961 to 1962 were coded as follows:

Pattern of Income Change '60 over '59, and '61 over '60	Expected Income Change 1962 Compared to 1961			
	Larger in 1962	Same both years	Smaller in 1962	Not ascertained
'59 > '60 > '61	C	C	*	E
'59 > '60 = '61	C	C	E	E
'59 > '60 < '61	D	C	D	E
'59 = '60 < '61	C	C	E	E
'59 = '60 = '61	B	B	A	E
'59 = '60 < '61	B	B	A	E
'59 < '60 > '61	D	A	D	E
'59 < '60 = '61	B	B	A	E
'59 < '60 < '61	B	A	A	E
Not ascertained any year	E	E	E	E

Groups

A Above normal income
B Normal income
C Below normal income
D Fluctuating income
E Not ascertained

*Too few cases to classify.

Chapter 6

Saving and Spending as Explained by all the Variables*

In previous chapters we have developed and investigated a number of variables that we believe have important effects on saving or spending decisions. Because these inquiries were often carried out within a specific model of consumer behavior and because they were conducted simultaneously, they could not make use of relevant findings in the other analyses. What remains to be done is to assess the relative importance of all the possible factors simultaneously. The purpose of this chapter is to present such an assessment.

We have not provided here a tight test of a single specific model but have instead selected from among many competing hypotheses those (explanatory variables) which are most important. For this purpose highly flexible multivariate procedures are desirable, procedures with minimal assumptions about linearity and additivity. We first made use of a newly developed automated process that searches for interaction effects and nonlinearities. After this process had been applied to the data, we created new variables and selected from the new and old variables a set to be used in ordinary dummy variable regression.[1]

An important consequence of this two stage procedure was the development of a classification based on a combination of self-employment, house value and total assets in early 1960. The classes

*This chapter was written by James N. Morgan.

[1] For the logical background and purpose of the process, see James N. Morgan and John A. Sonquist, "Problems in the Analysis of Survey Data, and a Proposal," *Journal of the American Statistical Association,* LVIII (June 1963), 415-34. For some results see James N. Morgan and John A. Sonquist, "Some Results from a Nonsymmetrical Branching Process that Looks for Interaction Effects," *Proceedings* of the 1963 Meetings, Social Statistics Section, American Statistical Association, (August, 1963), 40-53. For a complete program description and results and suggestions for its use see John A. Sonquist and James N. Morgan. *The Detection of Interaction Effects* (Ann Arbor, Mich.: Survey Research Center, 1964), Monograph 35, price $3.

were then converted into dummy variables. The next step was to introduce the explanatory variables into a dummy variable regression model which deserves a more detailed explanation.

Multiple regression techniques now implemented on large-scale computers can be made much more flexible by the use of "dummy variables."[2] Rather than assume linearity, or some restricted quadratic or log form, one may allow the data to determine the shape of the relationship between some explanatory or predictor variable, and the dependent variable. Thus, predictors that are ordered (or even unordered) classifications may be used in a conventional multiple regression model. Even when the explanatory factor has a numerical measure, such as income, little precision is lost when converting it to, say, ten classes; and much flexibility is gained since no assumptions need be made about the shape of its effect. Indeed, with most survey data, errors of measurement are large enough so that some of the lost precision is likely to be spurious anyway.

When the question arises as to the importance of various explanatory factors in reducing predictive error, or their level of significance, however, it is usually a *set* of dummy variables which is involved, not just a single one. For example, the usual question is not how important being a high school graduate is, but how important education is. Hence, one needs some measure analogous to the partial beta coefficient which is applicable to a complete set of dummy variables (including the one omitted to avoid overdetermination).

It is easier to see the logic of the measure proposed here if one approaches the problem indirectly. Suppose we convert the multiple regression results into a slightly different form in which each class of each characteristic has a coefficient, the weighted mean of each set is zero, and the constant term is the grand mean.

For three sets of dummy variables, we have the prediction equation:

(1) $\hat{Y}_\alpha = \overline{Y} + a_i + b_j + c_k + e$

[2] Each class, except one, of the explanatory characteristic is assigned a variable X_i which takes the value of one if the observation belongs in that class and zero if it does not. See Daniel Suits, "The Use of Dummy Variables in Regression Equations," *Journal of the American Statistical Association*, LII (December 1957), 548-51.

where a, b, and c are the coefficients of the i'th, j'th, etc., classes of predictors A, B, and C, respectively, and e is an error term. This is the form in which the variance analysis models are frequently given. The conversion of any set of dummy variables is straightforward. Suppose we have for the b_i's:

Group	Dummy variable regression coefficients	Proportion of sample	Adjusted coefficients
1. Open country	$b_1 = -10$	.2	$B_1 = -11$
2. Town	b_0 (omitted)	.5	$B_0 = -1$
3. City	$b_2 = +10$	.3	$B_2 = +9$

Each adjusted coefficient B_i is computed from:

(2) $B_i = b_i + Q$

where Q is an adjusting constant, determined from the equation:

(3) $.2(-10 + Q) + .5(0 + Q) + .3(10 + Q) = 0$

in order to make the weighted sum of the coefficients equal to zero. Generally, Q is computed from the formula:

$$(4)\quad \sum_{i=1}^{NC} P_i(b_i + Q) = 0$$

when NC is the total number of classes, including the omitted one and P_i is the corresponding proportion of the sample.

As a check, if the constant used for each set of dummy variables is obtained and these constants are summed and added to the constant term from the regression, then this should equal the mean of the dependent variable.

$$(5)\quad \sum_{i=1}^{NP} Q_i + A = \overline{Y}$$

Now suppose one considers the adjusted coefficients (B_i) as numbers. There is, then, a set of numbers for each explanatory characteristic. Any individual is assigned exactly one number for each characteristic, depending on the class in which he falls. If we used these numbers as a new set of variables and ran a multiple regression with the same dependent variable, it can be shown that the partial regression coefficient b_i for each of these new variables would be equal to 1.0, and the constant term of this regression equation would be the mean of the dependent variable.

The formula for the usual partial beta coefficient is:

$$(6) \quad \beta_i^* = b_i \frac{\sigma_i}{\sigma_y}$$

But with this set of new variables, b_i is always equal to 1.0, the standard deviation of the dependent variable is known, and the standard deviation of our artificial variable is nothing but the weighted sum of squares of the coefficients which became the variable. In this case, the beta coefficient for a set of dummy variables[3] is:

$$(7) \quad \beta_s^* = \frac{1}{\sigma_y} \sqrt{\frac{\sum_{i=1}^{NC} N_i B_i^2}{\Sigma N_i}}$$

In practice it is frequently advantageous to convert the dummy variable coefficients into the B-form so that there is one for each subclass, and they all become adjustments to the grand mean, as in formula (7).[4]

If one prefers the dummy variable coefficients excluding one class as they come from a regular regression using matrix inversion techniques, then the formula for the beta coefficient for the set becomes:

$$(8) \quad \beta_s = \frac{1}{\sigma_y} \sqrt{\frac{\Sigma N_i b_i^2 - (\Sigma N_i b_i)^2}{\Sigma N_i}}$$

where N is the number of observations in the i'th class of predictor s.[4] The reason for the differences between formulas (7) and (8)

---

[3] See Frank Andrews, "The Revised Multiple Classification Analysis Program" (Ann Arbor, Mich.: Survey Research Center, 1963), 13 pp. (mimeographed).

[4] For empirical results using this measure, see James N. Morgan, Martin David, Wilbur Cohen and Harvey E. Brazer, *Income and Welfare in the United States* (New York: McGraw-Hill, 1962).

lies in the fact that the B_i have a mean of 0, whereas the b_i do not.

Since the "variable" involved here is more flexible than the usual numerical variable, no sign attaches to these beta coefficients. In all other respects, however, they appear analogous to the usual partial beta coefficients and are subject to the same advantages and disadvantages. As a measure of the importance of a particular explanatory factor, relative to others, or to other regressions, this coefficient appears to be accepted as a reasonable measure. Of course, it falls short of the ideal procedure by which the data are reanalyzed omitting each factor in turn in order to see the amount by which the total explanatory power of the regression is reduced.

It is also possible to ignore sample complications and compute a crude F-test of the significance of a set of coefficients, using the unexplained sum of squares from the total regression as the denominator. However, with samples of 1000 or more, most sets with substantial beta coefficients will be significant anyway, and for others, the test provides no discrimination of patterns of coefficients which are frequently nonrandom, even when the beta coefficients are small.

It will be of value to begin the discussion of substantive results by presenting for each of our three dependent variables the ranking of explanatory variables according to their beta coefficient. Subsequently each explanatory variable will be discussed separately. It will be noted in Tables 6-1, 6-2, and 6-3 that the overall correlation coefficient is apparently quite low. Partly this is due to our regression model in which explanatory variables are coded 1 or 0, but largely because dividing by income removes most of the effect of the most important variable.

Table 6-4 shows dramatic differences between five subgroups of the sample in both total saving and discretionary saving. An entrepreneurial group saves most, even when one looks at the adjusted means which "take account" of all the other factors (in the multiple regression sense). This result is consistent with our findings in Chapter 5. Homeowners who started the period with substantial assets saved substantial fractions of their incomes, even after adjustments for income, age, and so forth. This could not have been merely the result of large mortgage payments, since their discretionary saving was also high. One implication is that homeowners tend to be savers, and the larger their asset values, the more they save. Thus, for this group assets serve as an additional proxy for a propensity to save that probably perseveres over time.

Table 6-1

CHARACTERISTICS USED TO EXPLAIN TWO-YEAR TOTAL SAVING
AS A PERCENTAGE OF TWO-YEAR INCOME

(For 953 spending units with two-year incomes of $2000 or more)

Characteristics of spending units	Relative importance of characteristic (beta coefficient)
Occupation, house value, and total assets held early in 1960	.244
Life cycle	.148
Two-year income (1960 and 1961)	.145
Pattern of reported and anticipated income 1959 through 1962 (normal income)	.121
Age of head	.103
Sources of income change 1960 to 1961	.100
Sources of income change 1959 to 1960	.100
Size of place of residence	.097
Changes in optimism index 1960 to 1962	.095
Anticipated income change 1961 to 1962	.078
Years lived at present address	.068
Educational attainment of head	.060
Course of income over past 10 years	.058
Anticipated course of income over next 10 years	.049

Correlation coefficient squared = .03

Table 6-2

CHARACTERISTICS USED TO EXPLAIN TWO-YEAR DISCRETIONARY SAVING
AS A PERCENTAGE OF TWO-YEAR INCOME

(For 953 spending units with two-year incomes of $2000 or more)

Characteristics of spending units	Relative importance of characteristic (beta coefficient)
Occupation, house value, and total assets held early in 1960	.241
Two-year income (1960 and 1961)	.136
Course of income over past 10 years	.131
Pattern of reported and anticipated income 1959 through 1962 (normal income)	.123
Changes in optimism index 1960 to 1962	.087
Age of head	.086
Life cycle	.085
Anticipated income change 1961 to 1962	.085
Sources of income change 1959 to 1960	.080
Size of place of residence	.076
Years lived at present address	.073
Sources of income change 1960 to 1961	.069
Educational attainment of head	.057
Anticipated course of income over next 10 years	.045

Correlation coefficients squared = .03

Table 6-3

CHARACTERISTICS USED TO EXPLAIN TWO-YEAR MAJOR CONSUMER INVESTMENT
EXPENDITURE AS A PERCENTAGE OF TWO-YEAR INCOME

Characteristics of spending units	Relative importance of characteristic (beta coefficient)
Life cycle	.251
Age of head	.200
Two-year income (1960 and 1961)	.158
Occupation, house value, and total assets held early in 1960	.133
Reported course of income over past 10 years	.124
Size of place	.122
Anticipated course of income over next 10 years	.110
Sources of income change 1960 to 1961	.089
Sources of income change 1959 to 1960	.086
Educational attainment of head	.077
Anticipated income change 1961 to 1962	.062
Pattern of reported and anticipated income 1959 through 1962 (normal income)	.060
Changes in optimism index 1960 to 1962	.050
Years lived at present address	.044

Correlation coefficient squared = .02

Table 6-4

TWO-YEAR SAVING AND EXPENDITURE RATES
BY OCCUPATION, HOUSE VALUE, AND TOTAL ASSETS HELD EARLY IN 1960

(In per cent)

Occupation, house value, and total assets held early in 1960	Number of cases	Two-year total saving rate		Two-year discretionary saving rate		Number of cases	Two-year major investment expenditure rate	
		Class mean	Adjusted mean[a]	Class mean	Adjusted mean[a]		Class mean	Adjusted mean[a]
Self-employed businessmen, artisans, farmers, and farm managers	121	27.1	28.9	21.1	23.3	120	9.4	9.0
Those who owned a house valued at $2500 or more and who had total assets of $25,000 or more[b]	85	19.6	16.3	17.0	13.3	83	8.8	8.0
Those who owned a house valued at $2500 or more and who had total assets of less than $25,000[b]	481	11.4	10.0	4.8	3.8	468	7.6	7.7
Those who do not own or who owned a house valued at less than $2500 and who had total assets of $1000 or more (or assets N.A.)[b]	98	-4.7	-2.7	-6.2	-5.2	98	5.2	5.5
Those who do not own or who owned a house valued at less than $2500 and who had less than $1000 of total assets (or assets (N.A.)[b]	168	5.1	8.5	2.9	5.5	165	5.6	5.6
Number of cases reporting data	953					934		
Grand mean		11.4		6.5			7.3	

[a]Mean of class observations after an additive adjustment has been made for the influence of explanatory variables discussed in this study.
[b]Excluding self-employed businessmen, artisans, farmers, and farm managers.

On the other hand, the nonowners not only save considerably less, but those who had any substantial assets at the beginning of the period tended to dissave. A commonly held proposition that assets encourage spending appears to be true, but only for part of the population—those who do not have a business or farm to encourage saving for investment purposes, and those who have not revealed a preference for saving through the purchase of a house and accumulation of assets.

The differences between the groups in expenditure rates on consumer investments (in cars, appliances and additions and repairs to the home) are largely differences between the first three groups who generally own their homes, and the last two, who do not. If one counted some part of these expenditures as saving (they do increase net worth to the extent that the results last more than a year), they are clearly not a substitute for other saving. Homeowners also have more depreciation on previous purchases, so that their saving is overstated somewhat more than that of renters. In other words, part of the differences between homeowners and renters is a result of conceptual and measurement problems. The same group who have more, however, also tend to invest slightly more in things which provide a stream of services.

Table 6-5 shows high rates of both saving and spending on durables among those in the middle stages of the family life cycle in spite of the financial pressures connected with raising children. The explanation lies in contractual saving among the middle aged (mortgage payments and life insurance) in the low incomes and mild responsibilities of the young single people and the old retired single people. However, a sharp reduction in spending on durables and a sharp increase in the rate of saving is exhibited for the group with children 6 years of age or older. Retired couples tend to save a lot and to spend more than expected for their income on cars, durables, additions and repairs. This reflects their substantial total investment in housing and household equipment. Merely to maintain a stock so disproportionately large relative to income requires substantial replacement expenditures.

Saving and durable expenditure rates vary markedly according to the spending unit's total two-year income (Table 6-6). The saving and expenditure rates depart from linearity and from each other in an apparently complicated way. Both adjusted and unadjusted saving rates exhibit a tendency to increase with two-year income, not without, however, exhibiting a tendency to decline between incomes of

Table 6-5

TWO-YEAR SAVING AND EXPENDITURE RATES
BY LIFE CYCLE

(In per cent)

Life cycle	Two-year total saving rate		Number of cases	Two-year discretionary saving rate		Number of cases	Two-year major investment expenditure rate	
	Class mean	Adjusted mean[a]		Class mean	Adjusted mean[a]		Class mean	Adjusted mean[a]
Unmarried								
Under age 45	-3.5	3.2	54	-3.6	-.3	34	6.3	5.1
Age 45 or over								
In labor force	9.7	6.8	77	6.5	4.0	76	6.2	6.6
Retired	3.1	4.3	54	2.3	4.6	53	5.0	8.5
Married								
Under age 45								
2 or more adults								
No children	12.5	15.1	27	5.7	5.6	27	6.7	5.7
Children:								
Youngest under 6	12.8	17.4	219	7.1	6.2	217	8.3	6.7
Youngest 6 or over	15.4	21.4	116	8.8	9.4	112	6.4	4.8
Age 45 or over								
2 or more adults								
Has children	12.0	8.3	149	5.4	3.6	144	6.1	6.8
No children:								
Not retired	12.1	10.0	150	6.6	4.2	145	8.4	5.3
Retired	19.6	21.0	73	17.4	17.4	73	9.5	12.8
Number of cases reporting data			919			881		
Grand mean	11.4			6.5			7.3	

[a]Mean of class observations after an additive adjustment has been made for the influence of explanatory variables discussed in this study.

Table 6-6

TWO-YEAR SAVING AND EXPENDITURE RATES
BY TWO-YEAR INCOME OF SPENDING UNIT (1960 AND 1961)

(In per cent)

Two-year income	Number of cases	Two-year total saving rate		Two-year discretionary saving rate		Number of cases	Two-year major investment expenditure rate	
		Class mean	Adjusted mean[a]	Class mean	Adjusted mean[a]		Class mean	Adjusted mean[a]
$2000 to 3999	89	12.8	11.2	8.4	4.9	89	4.3	5.2
$4000 to 5999	85	5.0	3.4	3.3	.5	83	8.5	8.4
$6000 to 7999	80	9.1	9.0	5.6	4.4	79	6.8	7.1
$8000 to 9999	107	6.0	5.3	2.8	1.1	106	8.2	8.8
$10,000 to 11,999	104	9.0	9.5	3.9	4.1	103	9.0	8.8
$12,000 to 14,999	156	11.8	13.4	5.2	7.5	158	7.0	6.8
$15,000 to 19,999	157	13.5	15.1	7.3	9.9	156	6.8	6.3
$20,000 to 29,999	108	19.5	19.3	13.3	14.1	100	8.0	7.1
$30,000 and over	38	19.1	15.4	13.9	12.5	37	5.4	4.6
Number of cases reporting data	924					906		
Grand mean		11.4		6.5			7.3	

[a]Mean of class observations after an additive adjustment has been made for the influence of explanatory variables discussed in this study.

$4000 and $12,000. Matching this decline in saving rates is the increase in the durable expenditure rate for spending units falling in these income classes. This pattern remains after adjustment for the multivariate character of the durable expenditure process. For those analysts who view saving and spending on durables as substitute activities of a high degree, there is some evidence in support of their view in these income classes. The apparent decline in both the rate of saving and spending on durables among spending units in the highest income group is probably a result of the small size of the sample.

In Chapter 3 we probed beneath reported income changes to describe causes for changes such as unemployment and wage and salary rate changes. At this point, we investigate another aspect of income change: whether income changes reported during 1960 and 1961 were expected by respondents to continue on into 1962. What we are interested in is the effect of the consumer's perception or appraisal of income change on spending and saving decisions. However, in the present study we have no direct information on this appraisal. We may exploit the panel character of the data, however, and distinguish subgroups with different patterns of reported and anticipated income change. Finally, we may ask whether different patterns of income change experience and anticipations are associated with different saving and durable spending behavior.

Since we have given an explicit account of the preparation of this variable in Chapter 5, the essential ideas involved in preparing the special income changes variable may be presented succinctly: those who expected their incomes to decline from 1961 to 1962 and who also reported at least one income increase (and no decreases) in the period 1959 to 1961 were treated as having experienced "above normal" income during the period 1960 and 1961. Another way of looking at this subgroup is to see them as being above their trend income position. Reversing the signs of these income change events yields another subsample who were treated as having experienced "below normal" income or as being below their trend position. The subsample who expected income changes in 1962 in the same direction as the income changes they reported from 1959 to 1960 and from 1960 to 1961 were treated as having experienced "normal" income, or as being on their income trend line. Those spending units with a pattern of reversals of direction of income change were treated as having experienced fluctuating incomes. This line of reasoning yields four distinct groups in the sample which are large enough to yield sample sizes of interest.

We may observe in Table 6-7 that the spending units classified as having fluctuating income experiences reported the highest saving rate and the lowest spending rate on durables as revealed by the class mean and the adjusted mean. This group contains a high proportion of self-employed and farmers who have a variety of motivations to save independent of income fluctuation. On the other hand, the effects of self-employment were presumably incorporated into the first predictor-set, and "held constant" by the regression.

For those spending units classified as having experienced "above normal" income, the average saving rate, both total and discretionary, is higher than the rates for those classified in the "normal" or "below normal" categories. The lowest average saving rates are reported for the group classified as "below normal income." There were reasons to believe that expenditure rates for durables would follow the same pattern, but they do not. They follow a reverse pattern, in fact, though the differences are small and more than covered by sampling error. The above normal group reports together with the group reporting fluctuating income the lowest spending rate. A slightly higher spending rate is reported for the "normal income" group, and a slightly higher rate for the "below normal income" group. The latter finding is a surprise, although it must be repeated that the differences among these rates are small. Perhaps some durables, at least, are necessities that have to be bought regardless of temporary financial stress.

Several conclusions may be drawn from these results. Those spending units who apparently enjoyed above normal income during the 1960-1961 period but who anticipated a decrease in 1962 from 1961 did not spend for durables on the average at a higher rate than others; in fact, if anything, they spent at a lower rate. The average saving rate was higher for this group and was markedly lower for the group classified as "below normal income." Thus, we find evidence supporting the views of those who regard the consumers' perception or appraisal of income changes as important determinants of saving and spending decisions. Our results are consistent with those reported by Katona in an earlier study in which a similar but finer classification of spending units with respect to income change was made.[5]

---

[5] George Katona, *The Powerful Consumer* (New York: McGraw-Hill Book Company, Inc., 1960), pp. 150-51.

Table 6-7

TWO-YEAR SAVING AND EXPENDITURE RATES
BY THE PATTERN OF INCOME CHANGES 1959 TO 1960, 1960 TO 1961
AND EXPECTED INCOME CHANGE 1961 TO 1962

(In per cent)

Trend of income changes[a]	Number of cases	Two-year total saving rate		Two-year discretionary saving rate		Number of cases	Two-year major investment expenditure rate	
		Class mean	Adjusted mean[b]	Class mean	Adjusted mean[b]		Class mean	Adjusted mean[b]
Fluctuating income experience (reversal of direction of income change during the period)	49	18.7	21.9	12.0	15.6	48	6.9	6.7
Respondent expected a decrease of income 1961 to 1962 reversing the trend of changes 1959 to 1960 and 1960 to 1961 (above normal income)	129	14.3	16.4	8.0	9.7	127	7.5	6.8
Respondent expected a continuation of income change 1961 to 1962 as reported from 1959 to 1960 and 1960 to 1961 (normal income situation)	558	11.4	10.2	6.8	5.8	550	7.2	7.2
Respondent expected an increase of income 1961 to 1962 reversing the trend of changes 1959 to 1960 and 1960 to 1961 (below normal income)	160	6.1	5.8	1.7	.7	155	7.3	7.7
Income experience not ascertained and miscellaneous changes	57	13.4	17.9	9.1	14.2	54	8.2	9.4
Number of cases reporting data	953					934		
Grand mean		11.4		6.5			7.3	

[a] Income changes 1959 to 1960 and 1960 to 1961 were calculated from income information provided by the respondent early in 1960, 1961, and 1962. Expected 1962 income was obtained early in 1962. The question was: "Do you expect your total family income in 1962 will be larger, smaller, or about the same as 1961?"

[b] Mean of class observations after an additive adjustment has been made for the influence of explanatory variables discussed in this study.

A marked nonlinear even parabolic influence of age upon the saving rates is suggested in Table 6-8 in which the saving rates decline in the brackets with heads of spending units aged 35 to 54 years. This parabolic pattern is not exhibited, however, by the durable expenditure rate. Rather the major expenditure rate declines steadily from age class to age class with perhaps a slight tendency to rise in the oldest age class. These results are consistent with the view that older consumers are more "stocked up" with durables. An important feature of these results is that they are more clearly exhibited after the dependent variable has been cleansed of the influence of other explanatory variables. One cautionary comment is required at this point: we have already noted that the durable expenditure rate examined by life cycle group rises for spending units which have retired heads and no children and this effect has been removed from the dependent variables. Consequently, our results in Table 6-8 are considered to be brought about by an independent age effect, life cycle stage being taken into account in the multivariate regression process.

The next two variables, sources of income change from 1959 to 1960 and from 1960 to 1961 presented in Tables 6-9 and 6-10 are fruitfully studied together. A rather striking feature of the results is the higher saving rates reported in both tables for those units which reported a reduced income and a reduced number of weeks worked. It is possible that these events (unemployment, illness) induced the spending unit to save at a higher rate for precautionary reasons. There is an imprecision in our income change variable that ought to be pointed out at this juncture as it may provide an alternative explanation of these higher saving rates. It is possible that other members of the spending unit experienced different income and employment events offsetting the events reported for the head. An interesting area for further research is opened up in which the sequence of income and employment events of the head of the spending unit may be combined with the income and employment events of other members of the spending unit.

Total and discretionary saving rates tended to be higher than the average for spending units in which the income of the head in 1961 and 1960 remained steady but in which the wife's income reportedly increased. The major expenditure rate is if anything lower for this group. Such a pattern is consistent with the view that when the wife first goes to work, more of the added income tends to be saved. Additional evidence on this pattern is obtained from the saving and

Table 6-8

TWO-YEAR SAVING AND EXPENDITURE RATES
BY AGE OF HEAD
(In per cent)

Age of head of unit	Number of cases	Two-year total saving rate		Two-year discretionary saving rate		Number of cases	Two-year major investment expenditure rate	
		Class mean	Adjusted mean[a]	Class mean	Adjusted mean[a]		Class mean	Adjusted mean[a]
Under 25	20	9.0	21.0	4.6	15.2	19	8.8	10.6
25-34	156	11.8	12.8	7.0	10.2	153	8.0	9.0
35-44	259	10.4	7.0	5.1	5.1	256	7.1	8.5
45-54	208	9.8	10.5	3.7	3.6	205	7.1	6.6
55-64	159	14.6	16.5	9.9	9.0	152	7.4	6.9
65 and over	151	11.7	11.9	9.1	5.1	149	6.9	4.4
Number of cases reporting data	953					934		
Grand mean		11.4		6.5			7.3	

[a]Mean of class observations after an additive adjustment has been made for the influence of explanatory variables discussed in this study.

Table 6-9

TWO-YEAR SAVING AND EXPENDITURE RATES
BY SOURCES OF INCOME CHANGE, 1959 TO 1960

(In per cent)

Sources of income change, 1959 to 1960	Number of cases	Two-year total saving rate		Two-year discretionary saving rate		Number of cases	Two-year major investment expenditure rate	
		Class mean	Adjusted mean[a]	Class mean	Adjusted mean[a]		Class mean[a]	Adjusted mean[a]
Head's earned income higher								
Does not report working more weeks	289	12.9	8.3	7.7	6.4	287	7.5	7.6
Reports working more weeks	89	8.4	8.9	5.3	7.6	85	6.8	7.6
Head's earned income lower								
Does not report working fewer weeks	267	13.5	12.9	8.1	6.2	263	7.9	7.6
Reports working fewer weeks	90	11.4	15.7	8.2	11.2	87	7.3	7.7
Head's earned income same (within ± 4%)								
Wife earned more	22	10.7	10.1	5.3	4.4	21	9.4	8.9
Wife earned less	20	7.6	7.4	.8	1.3	19	9.2	8.4
Head and wife earned same as previous year								
Total SU income greater	23	6.8	7.2	2.0	3.5	23	7.1	6.5
Total SU income smaller	12	17.6	18.6	7.3	10.1	12	2.9	2.2
None of above: spending unit income steady	113	5.1	4.9	.9	1.8	109	6.0	5.8
Number of cases	905					906		
Grand mean		11.4		6.5			7.3	

[a] Mean of class observations after an additive adjustment has been made for the influence of explanatory variables discussed in this study.

Table 6-10

TWO-YEAR SAVING AND EXPENDITURE RATES
BY SOURCES OF INCOME CHANGE, 1960 TO 1961

(In per cent)

Sources of income change 1960 to 1961	Number of cases	Two-year total saving rate		Two-year discretionary saving rate		Number of cases	Two-year major investment expenditure rate	
		Class mean	Adjusted mean[a]	Class mean	Adjusted mean[a]		Class mean	Adjusted mean[a]
Head's earned income higher								
Does not report working more weeks	297	13.7	12.2	8.0	7.4	291	8.1	7.9
Reports working more weeks	62	7.6	5.3	4.4	2.1	61	6.1	6.1
Head's earned income lower								
Does not report working fewer weeks	279	11.3	9.6	7.4	5.1	277	7.8	7.8
Reports working fewer weeks	74	10.1	12.8	7.5	9.5	72	6.7	6.9
Head's earned income same (within ± 4%)								
Wife earned more	21	17.0	21.8	11.7	17.0	21	5.1	6.4
Wife earned less	16	6.7	4.0	1.1	-.3	15	6.7	5.1
Head and wife earned same as previous year								
Total SU income greater	32	17.5	20.6	6.6	9.3	30	5.6	6.3
Total SU income smaller	10	9.7	15.1	6.1	11.7	10	5.0	5.6
None of above: spending unit income steady	126	7.9	12.9	2.7	7.1	122	6.0	6.4
Number of cases	917					899		
Grand mean		11.4		6.5			7.3	

[a]Mean of class observations after an additive adjustment has been made for the influence of explanatory variables discussed in this study.

expenditure rates observed for the group in which the head reported the same income but the wife reported a decrease in the period 1960 to 1961. For this group the total and discretionary saving rates are relatively low as is the expenditure rate for major durables.

Is the same pattern discernible if we examine types of income change 1959 to 1960? The group of spending units in which the head's income was reported steady during the period but the wife's income was reported to have increased exhibited a lower total and discretionary saving rate but a high expenditure rate on major durables, a pattern opposite to the one revealed by the group with comparable experience in the period 1960 to 1961. The sample sizes of these groups are small and we do not wish to push the analysis too far; however, the reversal in these results suggests a time sequence of events—perhaps a build-up of assets and subsequent purchase of major durables. Such an analysis of the time sequence of events requires a different treatment of panel data than we have attempted. A direction for future research is indicated.

One of our underlying motives in devising the "sources of income change" variable was to study whether an income change brought about by a wage or salary rate change was regarded by consumers in the same way as an income change brought about by the changes in number of weeks worked. Several unexpected elements frustrated our aim: one element being the two-year character of our dependent variables, and another element being the numerous ways income can change. For those heads reporting for 1960 that their incomes were higher than 1959 but the number of weeks worked was unchanged, the average saving rates were, if anything, a little lower than the group reporting a higher earned income and an increased number of weeks worked. We considered the first group to have experienced an increase in wage or salary rates, and the second group to have experienced less unemployment. This pattern of results is sharply reversed when we consider income changes from 1960 to 1961. For spending units in which the heads had apparently received wage or salary increases, the average saving rates were considerably higher than for spending units (also receiving higher income) in which the head put in more work effort in 1961 than in 1960. Since increased work effort is likely to take place after a period of unemployment, these latter results seem plausible, reflecting unemployment in the first year of the two-year period for which saving was measured.

What are we to make of the large number of cases in which heads reported a lower earned income but no apparent change in weeks worked? In both periods the number of such cases was large. Decreases in wage and salary rates were not common enough during the period 1960 to 1961 to explain the large number in these groups. In fact it is a widely held belief that wage and salary rates are inflexible downwards. Rather than finding that widely held belief to be inconsistent with our results, we have found, after a closer look at examples of spending units in this group, that causes for variation in income other than working fewer than 52 weeks one year or the other are more important than we thought. Variations in the amount of overtime worked were reported by some members of this group. In some cases it was a variation in the income received from second jobs held by the head of the spending unit which accounted for the decrease in income without any apparent change in weeks worked. A third major explanation of this phenomenon was discovered to be variation in the income of the self-employed including farmers. The number of weeks worked may not be closely related to the income (net) of this group. This rich variety of reasons underlying decreases in income make our constructed variable rather imprecise, an imprecision to which we wish to call the attention of the reader. However, there is no need to reject our preliminary results. In fact, we believe a more fruitful research design can now be constructed for additional study.

A variable describing the size of place in which the spending unit lived during the interview period is of interest for several reasons. Consumption opportunities are likely to vary directly with size of place. The amount of information about, and the stimulation to buy, commodities are likely to vary directly with size of place. For these reasons, it seems plausible to expect the saving rate to shift downward and the major expenditure rate to shift upward for spending units living in big cities. If these results were exhibited in fact in Table 6-11, it would be difficult to claim that our interpretation was the only one consistent with the facts. It is possible that price levels for immediate consumption vary directly with size of place while the price levels of future consumption (as reflected in the rate of interest) may not so vary so that we may find some differences in the allocation of income to saving and spending by size of place. As a matter of fact, the results revealed in Table 6-11 reveal several conflicting patterns.

It is appropriate to warn the reader at this point that our size-of-place variable is not constructed quite properly for our purposes. While the classification provides a rough index of the population of

Table 6-11

TWO-YEAR SAVING AND EXPENDITURE RATES
BY SIZE OF PLACE IN WHICH SPENDING UNIT LIVED

(In per cent)

Size of place in which spending unit lives[a]	Number of cases	Two-year total saving rate		Two-year discretionary saving rate		Number of cases	Two-year major investment expenditure rate	
		Class mean	Adjusted mean[b]	Class mean	Adjusted mean[b]		Class mean	Adjusted mean[b]
Central cities of the 12 largest metropolitan areas	120	3.9	8.2	2.2	3.5	119	4.9	5.2
Cities of 50,000 and over (exclusive of central cities of 12 largest metropolitan areas)	204	9.1	10.2	4.3	5.4	198	6.8	6.8
Urban places								
10,000 to 49,999	163	15.1	15.8	9.2	9.9	159	6.7	6.5
2500 to 9999	175	8.7	6.5	4.4	2.9	170	8.0	8.2
Rural areas								
In a metropolitan area	95	21.3	12.5	16.1	10.8	93	8.3	8.1
Not in a metropolitan area	196	12.8	10.1	7.7	4.6	195	8.8	8.6
Number of cases	953					934		
Grand mean		11.4		6.5			7.3	

[a] As reported in the 1960 Census.

[b] Mean of class observations after an additive adjustment has been made for the influence of explanatory variables discussed in this study.

the place of residence of the spending unit, it provides for a distinction between the central cities of standard metropolitan statistical areas and the outlying parts which breaks up market areas. That is, a city of 30,000 located in a metropolitan area is grouped with other cities of that population rather than with other parts of the metropolitan area. Having introduced this cautionary note, let us see what the results indicate.

On the average the group of spending units with the lowest saving rates are those who live in the central cities of the twelve largest metropolitan areas. This finding seems to be compatible with one of two points of view: (1) that consumption opportunities are more plentiful in these areas or (2) that the cost of living in these areas is higher. The expenditure rate for major durables for this group is also the lowest of all groups, a finding which is most easily explained by higher cost of living. Both saving rates and spending rates are higher for spending units living in the outlying parts of the twelve largest metropolitan areas. These differentials are found, it will be recalled, after subtracting from the dependent variable an element attributed to income and one related to home ownership.

For spending units living in urban places with populations of 10,000 to 49,999, saving rates increase again on the average compared with the first two groups, and the spending rate is somewhat lower compared to the second group. This result is in accord with our ideas about consumption possibilities. However, saving rates declined and the spending rates increased for spending units living in urban places of 2500 to 9999.

Our conclusion with respect to the size-of-place variable reflects the ambivalence of our results. On one hand, significant differences are discernible in saving and spending rates when spending units are classified by size of place. On the other hand, plausible interpretations are only partly consistent with the results. In further work on this point it may be fruitful to prepare a variable that comes closer to the population size of the local market in order to evaluate more carefully the ideas about consumption opportunities that we discussed earlier.

In Table 6-12 we examine the variation in the dependent variables associated with changes in a specially constructed optimism index. The optimism index assigns equal weights to the respondent's replies to six attitudinal questions and then combines these weights to give an ordinal ranking of degrees of optimism. From this information the sample has been divided into groups with generally steady index

Table 6-12

TWO-YEAR SAVING AND EXPENDITURE RATES
BY CHANGE IN RESPONDENT OPTIMISM AS REPORTED IN 1960, 1961, AND 1962

(In per cent)

Change in respondent optimism during the period	Number of cases	Two-year total saving rate		Two-year discretionary saving rate		Number of cases	Two-year major investment expenditure rate	
		Class mean	Adjusted mean[a]	Class mean	Adjusted mean[a]		Class mean	Adjusted mean[a]
Optimism high	124	16.3	12.8	11.0	8.8	121	8.0	7.7
Optimism medium	252	11.4	13.2	6.2	7.6	248	7.6	7.2
Optimism low	241	9.2	10.3	5.4	5.9	235	7.2	7.7
Optimism rising	173	16.6	15.1	10.7	9.3	170	6.6	6.7
Optimism falling	156	5.2	5.3	.6	.8	153	7.4	7.5
Number of cases reporting data	946					927		
Grand mean		11.4		6.5			7.3	

[a]Mean of class observations after an additive adjustment has been made for the influence of explanatory variables discussed in this study.

values for each of the three interviews and with rising or falling index values. What is the effect upon the dependent variables of this fivefold classification of the sample?

The highest saving rates and lowest expenditure rate are exhibited by the group with rising index numbers—those who became more optimistic *during the period.* The discretionary saving rate declines further on the average among the group reporting steady low optimism values so that a distinct pattern of association between saving rates and optimism index values emerges. The pattern is not so distinct with respect to spending rates, a finding which raises the question of just what kind of expenditure rates decline when saving rates increase. Because we do not have a complete account of all kinds of consumer transactions, we cannot deal with this question here although it deserves further attention. Having found that the level and rate of change of optimism influence discretionary saving rates, it is appropriate to turn our attention to a variable that reflects an anticipation of the respondent.

The short-run income anticipations of respondents do appear to contribute something new in terms of an explanation of saving decisions. This point takes on added meaning when we recall that many aspects of spending unit income have already been taken into account: (1) two-year income, (2) pattern of reported and anticipated income change 1959 through 1962, (3) sources of income change 1960 to 1961, and (4) sources of income change 1959 to 1960. The adjusted total and discretionary saving rates are lower for those expecting decreased incomes in 1962 compared to 1961; this is the most striking finding derived from Table 6-13. The result is not straightforward on a priori grounds. It is conceivable, for example, that spending units anticipating a decrease in income would save more out of a given income. If this effect was present, it was apparently swamped by other circumstances (e.g., a series of successive income decreases which are likely to characterize the income patterns of unskilled workers and older people).

It may be surprising to some that the highest saving rates on the average are reported by spending units which anticipated 1962 income to be about the same as 1961 income, but this result has been reported in prior studies of the Survey Research Center. It is consistent with the view that for a decision-making unit stability of income can facilitate the formulation and execution of savings decisions. This point has been largely ignored in those studies in which the variability of income has been cited as a cause for an increased

Table 6-13

TWO-YEAR SAVING AND EXPENDITURE RATES
BY ANTICIPATED CHANGE IN INCOME FROM 1961 TO 1962

(In per cent)

Anticipated change in income from 1961 to 1962[a]	Number of cases	Two-year total saving rate		Two-year discretionary saving rate		Number of cases	Two-year major investment expenditure rate	
		Class mean	Adjusted mean[b]	Class mean	Adjusted mean[b]		Class mean	Adjusted mean[b]
1962 income anticipated to be larger than 1961	324	10.3	11.7	4.8	7.0	319	7.1	6.9
1962 income anticipated to be about the same as 1961	521	12.1	12.5	7.6	8.2	511	7.3	7.6
1962 income anticipated to be smaller than in 1961	85	10.3	3.1	5.9	-.9	82	8.3	8.0
Number of cases reporting data	930					912		
Grand mean		11.4		6.5			7.3	

[a] The question was: "Do you expect your total family income in 1962 will be larger, smaller, or about the same as 1961?"
[b] Mean of class observations after an additive adjustment has been made for the influence of explanatory variables discussed in this study.

proportion of saving out of income without relating variability of income to other factors.[6] Consequently, we find this result of great interest. It will also be observed in this connection that those spending units which anticipated an increase in 1962 income over that of 1961 reported on the average slightly lower saving rates than those anticipating steady incomes during the period.

In Table 6-14 we present the results obtained after introducing an explanatory variable which reflects the "years lived in present housing unit" of the spending unit. In every instance but one, the saving rates were higher for those spending units reporting lengthier periods of residence. This pattern remains after adjustment for other explanatory variables. Consequently, we conclude that lower residential mobility of the spending unit is associated with higher saving rates except for a slight qualification in the case of those who reported that they had lived in their unit since 1959. Such a pattern may indicate only that moving is expensive and that moving expenditures compete with saving. However, a more basic explanation may be worth exploring. The longer a spending unit has lived in present housing, the longer it has had to stock up on durables. Length of residence reported by the respondent may also reflect home ownership status and its consequences in a more complicated way than we have been able to allow for in our simple model.

Educational attainment, presented as a variable in Table 6-15, appears to be related in an indirect way to saving rates. These rates are higher for spending units whose heads had a grammar school education or less, and also for spending units whose heads had a college degree. Adjustment for the multivariate nature of saving decisions does not alter these results. There is a slight tendency for the major expenditure rate to exhibit the opposite pattern. It may be recalled at this point that the relative importance of educational attainment as an explanation of the total saving rate as measured by the beta coefficient was .060 so that we are at this stage considering variables which were probably not making a significant contribution to a reduction of the unexplained variation of the saving or spending rates.

Again it must be noted that the variation in spending rates among

[6]For example, see the study of Malcolm R. Fisher, "Explorations in Savings Behavior," *Bulletin of the Oxford Institute of Statistics,* Vol. 18, No. 3 (August 1956), pp. 201-77.

Table 6-14

TWO-YEAR SAVING AND EXPENDITURE RATES
BY YEARS LIVED IN PRESENT HOUSING UNIT

(In per cent)

Years lived in present housing unit[a]	Number of cases	Two-year total saving rate		Two-year discretionary saving rate		Number of cases	Two-year major investment expenditure rate	
		Class mean	Adjusted mean[b]	Class mean	Adjusted mean[b]		Class mean	Adjusted mean[b]
Since 1939 or earlier	121	14.9	16.2	11.7	11.2	120	7.6	7.1
Since the period 1940-1949	193	12.2	12.6	7.1	7.4	188	7.6	7.1
Since the period 1950-1954	220	12.1	11.0	6.0	5.4	212	6.9	7.0
Since the period 1955-1958	295	9.3	9.1	4.7	4.6	292	7.5	7.8
Since 1959	112	9.1	10.9	5.1	6.1	110	7.0	7.0
Total cases reporting years of residence and savings	941					922		
Grand mean		11.4		6.5			7.3	

[a]The question was: "About when did you move into (buy) this house (apartment)?"

[b]Mean of class observations after an additive adjustment has been made for the influence of explanatory variables discussed in this study.

Table 6-15

TWO-YEAR SAVING AND EXPENDITURE RATES
BY EDUCATIONAL ATTAINMENT OF HEAD OF SPENDING UNIT

(In per cent)

Educational attainment of head of spending unit	Number of cases	Two-year total saving rate		Two-year discretionary saving rate		Number of cases	Two-year major investment expenditure rate	
		Class mean	Adjusted mean[a]	Class mean	Adjusted mean[a]		Class mean	Adjusted mean[a]
Grammar school education or less (0-8 years)	264	11.9	12.8	7.7	8.0	259	6.3	6.2
Grammar school and some high school or noncollege schooling (9-11 years)	199	8.7	8.4	4.0	4.0	196	8.0	7.6
Completed high school (with or without added noncollege schooling)	235	9.8	6.4	5.0	6.3	230	7.8	7.7
College, no degree	105	13.4	13.0	7.8	6.2	103	7.8	8.3
College degree	144	15.3	14.5	9.4	8.3	140	7.0	7.2
Number of cases reporting data	947					928		
Grand mean		11.4		6.5			7.3	

[a]Mean of class observations after an additive adjustment has been made for the influence of explanatory variables discussed in this study.

the educational groups is small. We must confess again that our ability to explain the two-year expenditure rate on major durables has been very limited in this study. In fact, much of the variation in the spending rate is not statistically significant. It may be that, for this variable, averaging of expenditures over two years has succeeded only in removing the meaningful variation. We shall take up this topic again at the end of this chapter to discuss results obtained with a similar dependent variable prepared over a one-year period.

Of marginal statistical interest but of some theoretical interest is the influence upon saving rates of anticipations of income over the long-run future. In a similar category is the question of whether the way in which respondents perceive the trend of their incomes over a long period in the past has any influence upon their saving and spending decisions. Tables 6-16 and 6-17 may be considered together in this connection. A pattern may be detected. The highest saving rates were associated with incomes that declined steadily over the past ten years. The lowest saving rates were associated, generally, with incomes that rose steadily over the past ten years. Keeping readily at hand the knowledge that this pattern is not statistically different from no pattern at all, we may still express some interest in these results. It appears as if spending units with steadily declining incomes may have been led to higher saving rates in an effort to minimize the effect of income declines. This group also spent for durables on the average less than the other groups. These experiencing rising incomes in the past on the other hand may be undertaking relatively high consumption expenditures. We have made an additive allowance for age and life cycle, it will be noted. Income experience reported for the past ten years was not highly correlated with the anticipated course of income over the next ten years so that we may expect something different to emerge. Spending units anticipating rising incomes also tended to report a relatively higher adjusted discretionary saving rate and the highest adjusted durable expenditure rate. Saving rates tended to be lower on the average for those spending units that anticipated falling incomes, a result not at all consistent with the view that these units were attempting to build up assets in the face of anticipated declines.

In attempting to minimize panel losses, asset and debt balances were not asked in the middle interview, so that saving could be calculated only for the two-year period. The preceding analysis of two-year saving and investment expenditures has suffered from the problem, therefore, that the time dynamics are obscured by overlaps.

Table 6-16

TWO-YEAR SAVING AND EXPENDITURE RATES
BY INCOME EXPERIENCE OVER THE PAST TEN YEARS

(In per cent)

Income experience over the past ten years[a]	Number of cases	Two-year total saving rate		Two-year discretionary saving rate		Number of cases	Two-year major investment expenditure rate	
		Class mean	Adjusted mean[b]	Class mean	Adjusted mean[b]		Class mean	Adjusted mean[b]
Income has been going up steadily	478	9.8	9.8	4.5	4.8	464	7.8	6.7
Income has been going neither up nor down, has been steady	132	12.5	12.9	7.7	5.6	131	7.1	6.9
Income has been going down steadily	40	26.9	25.8	22.2	19.7	39	5.2	5.5
Income has been going down with fluctuations	40	7.8	11.3	2.6	4.1	40	8.7	8.0
Income has been fluctuating, no trend	179	13.2	11.1	8.5	6.8	176	6.8	6.7
Number of cases reporting data	829					850		
Grand mean		11.4		6.5			7.3	

[a] The question asked early in 1961 was: "Has your income been quite steady during the last ten years or so, or has it been going up, or down, or changing from time to time?" For younger respondents the question was: "Since you began working full-time, has your income been going up, or down, or changing from time to time?"

[b] Mean of class observations after an additive adjustment has been made for the influence of explanatory variables discussed in this study.

Table 6-17

TWO-YEAR SAVING AND EXPENDITURE RATES
BY INCOME ANTICIPATIONS OVER THE NEXT TEN YEARS

(In per cent)

Income anticipations over the next ten years[a]	Number of cases	Two-year total saving rate		Two-year discretionary saving rate		Number of cases	Two-year major investment expenditure rate	
		Class mean	Adjusted mean[b]	Class mean	Adjusted mean[b]		Class mean	Adjusted mean[b]
Income will go up	496	11.6	11.8	6.2	7.1	488	7.9	8.1
Income will stay about the same	104	12.9	12.2	7.0	6.5	98	6.2	6.9
Income will fall (including will retire)	55	9.4	9.0	6.5	5.6	54	8.4	7.8
Income will fluctuate	52	16.2	10.8	9.7	5.3	51	7.3	6.9
Answer not available or inappropriate: head is retired or a housewife	246					243		
Number of cases reporting data	953					934		
Grand mean		11.4		6.5			7.3	

[a]The question asked early in 1961 was: "During the next ten years or so, do you think your earnings will rise gradually, go up and down from year to year, or fall, or what?"

[b]Mean of class observations after an additive adjustment has been made for the influence of explanatory variables discussed in this study.

Many of the changes in conditions facing a family, or in its attitudes, occur during the period, rather than before it starts.

Consumer investment expenditures on cars, durables, and additions and repairs to homes were measured for each year, however, and an analysis was made of the expenditure for 1961 as influenced by various things that happened before then, including such things as the change in optimism from early 1960 to early 1961.

Definition of the Dependent Variable

Instead of eliminating the income effect in large part by division of the dependent variable by income it was decided to use the dollar expenditure as the dependent variable. And instead of taking first differences in time, that is, the change in expenditure over the previous year, it was decided to include the previous year's expenditure as one of the explanatory variables. The assumption was, of course, that while some people spend more than others year after year, the net effect of spending a great deal in any one year should be a reduction in expenditures the next year. To preserve comparability with the other multivariate results, however, those with two-year total incomes of less than $2000 were again omitted from the analysis.

The Explanatory Variables

The most important variables that have been shown to be of obvious importance in earlier analyses are (1) two-year total income and (2) the combination of occupation, house value and total assets early in 1960. Other variables have been created and explained in this monograph and an attempt has been made to test the hypotheses that changes in attitudes, or the different sources of changes in income will affect consumer spending behavior. The logic behind including education, stage in the family life cycle, income anticipations, and a pattern of recent and expected income changes should be plain.[7]

[7]Our dependent variable is highly aggregated over many kinds of commodities and for that reason, as well as to avoid using variables at different stages in the causal process, we shall not introduce buying plans for specific commodities as an explanatory variable into our equations. Buying plans have been found to be highly significant in cross-section studies. See, for example, Lawrence R. Klein and John B. Lansing, "Decisions to Purchase Consumer Durable Goods," *Journal of Marketing* (October 1955), Table II, p. 113.

The results of the analysis, in the form of partial beta coefficients for the sets of dummy variables involved, are given in Table
6-18. The analysis accounted for 17 per cent of the variance, much
of it attributable to income, of course. The influence of the various
explanatory factors will be discussed in conjunction with the tables
showing their detailed effects. These tables present the actual subgroup mean expenditures for each subclass of each predictor, and
then the "adjusted" means. The latter are what the mean would be if
that subgroup were like the whole sample on every other characteristic. They are the "dummy variable" regression coefficients with
the constant term added in.[8]

Income

The powerful and almost linear effect of income, revealed in
earlier studies, is shown in Chart 6.1 together with the relatively
small adjustments for the differential effects of other factors. (Among
the lowest income group—which has been excluded in our study—this
linear influence does not hold.)

Occupation, House Value, and Total
Assets in Early 1960

The combination of entrepreneurial status, home ownership and
initial assets used here (Table 6-19) came out of data searches in the
analysis of saving, where it was found that the initial possession of
assets led to higher saving for home owners, but less saving for
renters. The coefficients would make it appear that the amount of
investment expenditures is related in the same way to the various
combinations of initial asset possession and home ownership. In
other words the previous differences in saving measures which excluded investment in physical assets would be accentuated if we

---

[8]The regression coefficients for each set are first constrained so that their
weighted mean is zero, rather than the usual procedure of assigning a value of
zero to one and expressing the others as differences from it. Subtracting the mean
of $597 from any adjusted mean provides an estimate of the net effect on expendi-
tures of belonging to that group.

Table 6-18

CHARACTERISTICS USED TO EXPLAIN MAJOR INVESTMENT EXPENDITURES
DURING 1961

(For 1001 spending units with two-year incomes of $2000 or more)

Characteristics of spending units	Relative importance of characteristics in explaining expenditures (beta coefficient)
Two-year income (1960 and 1961)	.291
Occupation, house value, and total assets held early in 1960	.149
Sources of income change 1959 to 1960	.109
Size of place of residence	.096
Changes in optimism index 1960 to 1961	.089
Patterns of reported and anticipated income 1959 through 1962 (normal income)	.088
Sources of income change 1959 to 1961	.078
Educational attainment of head	.076
Anticipated course of income over next 10 years	.065
Anticipated income change 1961 to 1962	.065
Life cycle	.056
Years lived at present address	.053
Expressed satisfaction with saving	.053
1960 major investment expenditures ($50 or more = 1, less than $50 = 0)	.020

Chart 6-1

MAJOR EXPENDITURES BY TWO-YEAR AVERAGE INCOME

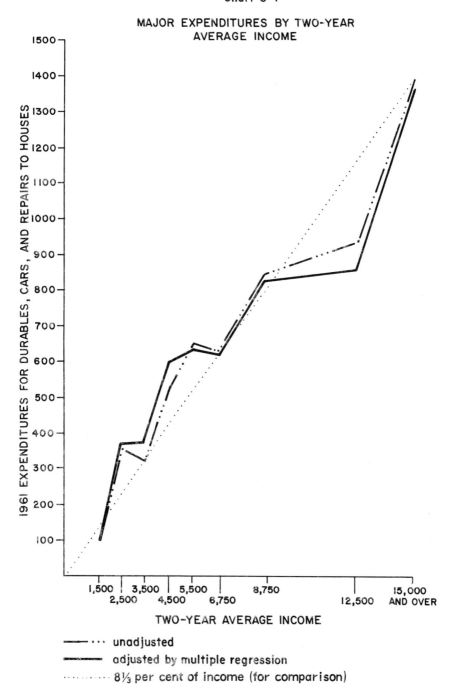

TWO-YEAR AVERAGE INCOME

——— ··· unadjusted

——— adjusted by multiple regression

·········· 8⅓ per cent of income (for comparison)

Table 6-19

MAJOR INVESTMENT EXPENDITURES DURING 1961 BY ENTREPRENEURIAL STATUS,
HOMEOWNERSHIP, AND TOTAL ASSETS HELD IN EARLY 1960

Entrepreneurial status, homeownership, and total assets held early in 1960	Number of cases	Average expenditures		Net effect[b] (in dollars)
		Class mean[a] (in dollars)	Adjusted mean[a] (in dollars)	
Self-employed business owners and farmers	137	774	685	88
Homeowners				
Total assets (early 1960)				
$25,000 or more	91	846	748	151
Less than $25,000	499	676	663	66
Nonowners				
Total assets (early 1960)				
$1000 or more	102	287	328	-269
Less than $1000	172	279	415	-182

[a] These values are not deviations from the grand mean.
[b] These values are deviations from the grand mean of $597.

included that investment in the measures of saving. Since their saving and investment expenditures are lowest, the residual, or down-the-drain expenditures are clearly *highest* for nonowners who started the period with some assets. Saving and investment are highest, and consumption or down-the-drain expenditures are lowest, for owners who started the period with some assets.

As discussed in Chapter 5, the influence of liquid assets upon saving is complicated: two conflicting hypotheses about the relation of initial assets to saving both appear to be true, but for different groups in the population. For some, identified here by their home ownership, assets are a measure of ability and willingness to save, and are associated with further high saving. For others, assets appear to be accumulated to buy things, and high initial assets lead to dissaving. Further investigation is needed before we consider the implications of this finding for policies about differential tax advantages for homeowners, but clearly no simple aggregate estimates of the effects of wealth on saving are justified.

Sources of Change in Income

The next most important explanatory factor was the type of income change experienced between 1959 and 1960, the two years before the 1961 period started! To facilitate comparisons, Table 6-20 combines these results with those for the sources of change in income between 1960 and 1961.

The most interesting thing is the differences in effects between the two time periods. Almost any kind of *change* between 1959 and 1960 seems to be associated with higher investment expenditures in 1961, yet the very highest spending in 1961, other things accounted for, seems to be among spending units in which the income of the head did not change between 1959 and 1960.

Focusing on the 1960 to 1961 change which should be the most relevant, we find that the second and fourth groups, which respectively recovered from and fell into unemployment, both reveal lower spending. One implication of this finding is that the uncertainty associated with changing availability of work inhibits the commitments involved in investment expenditures, even when things are looking better and income is higher. When other income fell (groups six and eight), investment spending was even lower. In general, moreover, the notion that the first group, which enjoyed increases in

Table 6-20

MAJOR INVESTMENT EXPENDITURES DURING 1961, BY SOURCES OF INCOME CHANGE

Sources of income change	1959 to 1960 change				1960 to 1961 change			
	Number of cases	Average expenditures		Net effect[a] (in dollars)	Number of cases	Average expenditures		Net effect[a] (in dollars)
		Class mean (in dollars)	Adjusted mean (in dollars)			Class mean (in dollars)	Adjusted mean (in dollars)	
Head has higher earned income								
Does not report working more weeks (full or part time) or more full time weeks	304	678	590	-7	309	736	640	43
Reports working more weeks, either full time or full time plus part time	91	544	663	66	64	580	489	-108
Head has lower earned income								
Does not report working fewer weeks (full or part time) or fewer full time weeks	286	542	611	14	301	520	599	2
Reports working fewer weeks, either full time or full plus part time	94	576	746	149	78	349	553	-44
Head has same earned income (within ± 4%)								
Wife earned more (whether from starting work, working more, or earning more per hour)	21	933	769	172	23	697	618	21
Wife earned less (whether from leaving labor force, working less, or getting less per hour)	20	955	854	257	17	489	338	-259
Head and wife earned same as previous year								
Total spending unit income greater (other sources provided more)	23	675	539	-58	32	735	567	-30
Total spending unit smaller	13	527	371	-226	10	326	370	-227
None of the above SU income changed less than ± 4%	19	525	425	-172	126	576	556	-41
Sources of income change not available	30	317	399	-198	41	627	805	208

[a] These values are deviations from the grand mean of $597.

rates of pay (or some extra, presumably voluntary, work) would be the *most* willing to commit itself to the future by spending on durable investment items, is borne out by the data particularly if one compares their +41 with the -41 of the group with *no* change in income.

The impression gained from the results for the first six groups that investment expenditures are expansible when income goes up and postponable when it goes down must be tempered by the fact that the multivariate analysis also includes variables reflecting the normalcy of income, and short- and long-run income expectations. The correlation between these measures of income dynamics, may have distorted the statistical results to some extent. Earlier studies left the impression that investment expenditures were sticky downward and explosibly flexible upward.[9] But perhaps times have changed.

Size of Place where Family Lives

After adjusting for differences in income, home ownership, and other factors, it is clear that consumer investment expenditures are lowest in the larger cities (Table 6-21). Although we have previously discussed this variable in some detail, several additional comments are now in order.

1. Better public transportation in larger cities makes cars somewhat less necessary; they are also more expensive to maintain in these areas. Big-city landlords are more likely to furnish the major appliances needed by tenants.

2. Consumer investment expenditures vary with the region in which the consumer lives: They tend to increase from the Northeast to the West. This result may be due to effects on durable inventories of population growth in the West.[10]

Change in Optimism from Early 1960
to Early 1961

Here for the first time is a clean test of the effect of prior *changes* in attitude. The differences in the adjusted averages are

[9]James N. Morgan, "Consumer Investment Expenditures," *American Economic Review*, XLVIII (December 1958), 874-902.

[10]Lawrence R. Klein and John B. Lansing, "Decisions to Purchase Consumer Durable Goods," *Journal of Marketing* (October 1955), p. 117.

probably not quite statistically significant, but they do show a tendency for increased optimism to be associated with higher spending, even after taking account of income, previous spending, and *past and expected income changes* (Table 6-22).

Interestingly enough, the group that was in the middle range both times (like the group with no income changes) spent relatively little. On the other hand, increased pessimism does not appear to be associated with very low investment expenditures in the following period. Nor does a return from pessimism to a middle position appear to lead to greater investment in future consumption. This may be the result of incorporating all kinds of income change and income expectations into other variables in the same analysis.

Income Situation, Above or Below Normal

We had thought that since the two-year saving rate depended in a significant and plausible way upon the normal situation, the major expenditures during 1961 would also depend upon these circumstances but in an inverse way. Our expectation was not borne out. After adjustment for the other explanatory variables, our results show that consumers in normal income situations tend to spend more than consumers in "abnormal" income situations (Table 6-23).

One interpretation of this finding is that investment expenditures are depressed by either past or expected declines in income, even if (as in the "below normal" case) the past decline has already been reversed.

Another interpretation is that income increases stimulate spending unless they are preceded or followed by decreases. We shall soon see that another variable representing expected change in income in 1962 shows a *positive* effect of expected *declines* on consumer investments, however.

We are, it should be noted, attempting to explain annual investment expenditures with a variable constructed over a three-year period, a variable that purports to place consumers on their (subjective) income trend position. These expenditures are the most volatile of all consumer expenditures--which lends to them a special interest. The point is that variables measured over the short run would seem more important in explaining investment fluctuations than a variable such as normal income.

Table 6-21

MAJOR INVESTMENT EXPENDITURES DURING 1961,
BY SIZE OF CITY

Size of place (by 1960 Census)	Number of cases	Average expenditures		
		Class mean (in dollars)	Adjusted mean (in dollars)	Net effect[a] (in dollars)
Central cities of the 12 largest metropolitan areas	128	458	478	-119
Other standard metropolitan areas (50,000 or more)	207	558	548	-49
Urban places				
10,000 to 49,999	172	617	552	-45
2500 to 9999	185	636	563	-34
Rural areas				
In a sampling unit (county) containing a standard metropolitan area	98	743	584	-13
In a sampling unit that does not contain a standard metropolitan area	211	606	584	-13

[a]These values are deviations from the grand mean of $597.

Table 6-22

MAJOR INVESTMENT EXPENDITURES DURING 1961,
BY CHANGE IN OPTIMISM FROM EARLY 1960 TO EARLY 1961

Change in optimism early 1960 to early 1961	Number of cases	Average expenditures		
		Class mean (in dollars)	Adjusted mean (in dollars)	Net effect[a] (in dollars)
Optimistic both times	63	777	610	13
Up from middle (or from pessimistic) to optimistic	92	816	723	126
Middle both times	264	606	564	-33
Down from optimistic to middle	107	770	681	84
Up from pessimistic to middle	113	379	407	-190
Pessimistic both times	140	492	608	11
Down to pessimistic from optimistic or from middle	222	539	630	33

[a]These values are deviations from the grand mean of $597.

Table 6-23

MAJOR INVESTMENT EXPENDITURES DURING 1961,
BY PATTERN OF INCOME CHANGE REPORTED 1959 TO 1960,
1960 TO 1961, AND ANTICIPATED 1961 TO 1962

| Level of 1960-61 income[a] | Number of cases | Average expenditures | | Net effect[b] (in dollars) |
		Class mean (in dollars)	Adjusted mean (in dollars)	
Above normal	129	642	460	-137
Normal	584	645	634	37
Below normal	174	460	549	-48
Income fluctuates	51	532	483	-114
Data not available	63	495	519	78

[a]Based on reported income changes 1959-1960, 1960-1961, and whether respondent expected total family income in 1962 to be larger, smaller, or about the same as 1961.

[b]These values are deviations from the grand mean of $597.

Table 6-24

MAJOR INVESTMENT EXPENDITURES DURING 1961,
BY EDUCATION OF HEAD OF SPENDING UNIT

| Education of head of unit | Number of cases | Average expenditures | | Net effect[a] (in dollars) |
		Class mean (in dollars)	Adjusted mean (in dollars)	
8 years of schooling or less	280	371	534	-63
Some high school (9-11 years)	205	604	629	32
High school graduate (12 years; some with additional noncollege schooling)	253	616	562	-35
Some college	104	778	708	111
College degree	152	856	671	74
Not ascertained	7	--	--	--

[a]These values are deviations from the grand mean of $597.

Education of Head of Unit

Even after adjustments for the differences in long-range expectations, home ownership, and income and income change that go with education, the respondents with more formal education appear more willing to commit their future consumption patterns by investing in durables and cars and additions and repairs.[11] One might speculate on the possibility that the large positive net effects in the second and fourth groups reflect the aspirations that led them to start high school or college in the first place and also the absence of the income that would have been theirs if they had completed their programs.

Ten-Year Earnings Expectations

Table 6-25 shows no particular effect from expecting higher or lower earnings over the next ten years, but it does show that uncertainty (and perhaps worry) about future earnings has a substantial depressing effect on expenditure. Moreover, it is likely that such long-run anticipations have little bearing on major investments as they are defined in our study. It is more likely that these long-run anticipations have a bearing on the purchase of housing.

Expected Change in Family Income from 1961 to 1962

Shorter range income expectations are held with less uncertainty, and might be expected to have more influence on current investment expenditures. The 1962 expectation variable, it should be noted, is built into the previously discussed index indicating whether current income was above or below normal. So there is a degree of correlation between these two explanatory variables that obscures their separate effects. Table 6-26 below shows that they are opposite to what the simple expectation theory would predict. One interpretation is that those who expect more income are holding off investing it, while those who expect less have already assured themselves against

---

[11]They also spend more on housing. See James N. Morgan, "Housing and Ability to Pay," *Econometrica* (in press).

Table 6-25

MAJOR INVESTMENT EXPENDITURES DURING 1961,
BY EXPECTED EARNINGS OVER THE NEXT TEN YEARS

| Expected earnings over the next ten years | Number of cases | Average expenditures | | Net effect[a] (in dollars) |
		Class mean (in dollars)	Adjusted mean (in dollars)	
Rise gradually, rise	516	728	622	25
Stay the same, about same	110	514	584	-13
Fall gradually, will retire	57	591	609	12
Go up and down, fluctuate	55	723	619	22
Don't know, not ascertained	108	371	437	-160
Retired, housewife	155	336	622	25

[a]These values are deviations from the grand mean of $597.

Table 6-26

MAJOR INVESTMENT EXPENDITURES DURING 1961
EXPECTED INCOME CHANGE FROM 1961 TO 1962

| Expected income change from 1961 to 1962[a] | Number of cases | Average expenditures | | Net effect[b] (in dollars) |
		Class mean (in dollars)	Adjusted mean (in dollars)	
Larger in 1962	339	626	524	-73
Same	548	583	573	24
Smaller in 1962	89	632	707	110
Not ascertained	25	397	675	78

[a]The question was: "Do you expect your total family income in 1962 will be larger, smaller, or about the same as in 1961?"

[b]These values are deviations from the grand mean of $597.

wasting their high current income by investing it in durables and other things that will last. A negative but hardly significant relation between short run income expectations and major investment expenditures has been reported in the study of Klein and Lansing already cited so that we are not surprised at these results nor are we very sure as to the most useful interpretation.[12]

Stage in the Family Life Cycle

Consumer investments build a stock of consumer capital and their timing should be affected by such things as marriage, the arrival of children, and perhaps a replacement cycle when the children leave home. Table 6-27 shows the pattern, in the order in which most people pass through the stages. The young married people with no children spend a lot, but not relatively to their high incomes which commonly involve two earners. And the older people who have a stock of capital spend less, after account is taken of their income and home ownership.

Satisfaction with Savings

Whatever the pattern of past or expected income changes, individuals may have their own notions whether their savings are adequate or whether they need to be increased. Presumably one way to increase them would be to postpone expenditures, and those on consumer investments are frequently quite postponable. The results, in Table 6-28, are the reverse of this expectation. The people who appear the least satisfied with their savings proceed to spend the most on consumer investment items during the subsequent year. Those who express no opinion are quite likely those most concerned about the adequacy of their savings, and they likewise spend a lot on consumer investment items. Perhaps consumers do treat these things like investments, or perhaps people who do not save worry but do not do anything about it.

[12]Klein and Lansing, *op. cit.*, Table IX, p. 119.

Table 6-27

MAJOR INVESTMENT EXPENDITURES DURING 1961
BY LIFE CYCLE

| Life cycle | Number of cases | Average expenditure | | Net effect[a] (in dollars) |
		Class mean (in dollars)	Adjusted mean (in dollars)	
Under age 45				
Unmarried, no children	55	363	622	25
Married, 2 or more adults, no children	27	689	538	-59
Married, 2 or more adults, children, youngest child under 6	224	765	645	48
Married, 2 or more adults, children, youngest child 6 or over	120	773	671	74
Age 45 or over				
Married, 2 or more adults, has children	159	613	512	-85
Married, 2 or more adults, no children; head in labor force	165	655	566	-31
Married, 2 or more adults, no children; head retired	78	426	542	-55
Unmarried, head in labor force	80	381	610	13
Unmarried, head retired	60	252	596	-1
Other				
Other; N.A. single adults with children	33	320	673	76

[a]These values are deviations from the grand mean of $597.

Table 6-28

MAJOR INVESTMENT EXPENDITURES DURING 1961
BY SATISFACTION WITH SAVINGS EARLY IN 1961

| Satisfaction with savings early in 1961[a] | Number of cases | Average expenditures | | Net effect[b] (in dollars) |
		Class mean (in dollars)	Adjusted mean (in dollars)	
Fully adequate	104	738	681	-16
Fairly satisfactory	167	655	608	11
Depends, maybe	6	--	--	--
Somewhat too little, not quite satisfactory	15	692	678	81
Too little, not satisfactory	336	671	619	2
Not ascertained	18	517	704	107
Has no reserves	355	469	576	-21

[a]The question was: "How do you feel about the amount you now have of these (savings, investments, or reserve funds), is it far too little, fairly satisfactory, fully adequate or what?"
[b]These values are deviations from the grand mean of $597.

Expenditures in the Preceding Year, 1960

The dynamics of spending are difficult to untangle in a cross section. There will always be gross positive correlations between spending in one year and spending in the next year because higher income, younger families are spending more. These are classic spurious correlations. Presumably hidden by these positive correlations is a negative effect by which spending a lot in one year depresses spending in the next year. This was the reason for including as an explanatory variable, whether the unit spent more than $50 in 1960 on consumer investment items. The results, while not significant statistically, point toward the implication that *after adjustments* for income, stage in the life cycle, etc., there is indeed a tendency for those who spend in one year to spend less the next year (Table 6-29).

How Long Lived in this Residence

Other studies have made much of the impact of moving on consumer investment expenditures. It has been found that recent movers tend to spend more on the durables included in our measure of major investments. Several reasons may account for this result: for one reason movers tend to be younger and at the stage at which durable inventories are being built-up, and for another reason, the fact of moving itself may create needs for these expenditures. In our panel, of course, there are no units which have moved recently. Consequently there is left only a mild tendency for those who moved in 1959, or who moved ten years ago, to invest more currently (Table 6-30).

Summary

A multivariate analysis explaining consumer investment expenditures in 1961 has confirmed some hypotheses, but caused a rethinking of many others. A number of the results would seem to indicate that far from competing with saving, these investment expenditures are associated with the same things that seem to lead to high savings. A theory which started with the assumption that people first had to accumulate a stock, and one proportionate to their

Table 6-29

MAJOR INVESTMENT EXPENDITURES DURING 1961
BY MAJOR INVESTMENT EXPENDITURES DURING 1960

Whether spent $50 or more on consumer investment items in 1960	Number of cases	Average expenditures		Net effect[a] (in dollars)
		Class mean (in dollars)	Adjusted mean (in dollars)	
Yes	254	790	568	-29
No	747	531	607	10

[a]These values are deviations from the grand mean of $597.

Table 6-30

MAJOR INVESTMENT EXPENDITURES DURING 1961
BY LENGTH OF RESIDENCE IN PRESENT HOUSING UNIT

About when did you move into (buy) this house (apartment)?	Number of cases	Average expenditures		Net effect[a] (in dollars)
		Class mean (in dollars)	Adjusted mean (in dollars)	
1939 or earlier	130	434	550	-47
1940-49	201	570	599	2
1950-54	231	562	615	18
1955-58	309	632	593	-4
1959	118	666	658	61
1960	12	196	562	-35

[a]These values are deviations from the grand mean of $597.

income, and then assumed that these accumulations were seen as making the family better off in the long run, i.e., as a place to invest temporarily high incomes, would fit the results better than a theory which treats these expenditures as consumption. Income increases not preceded or followed by decreases, seem to stimulate investment expenditures, as decreases, particularly with unemployment, inhibit them. Increased optimism, and high levels of optimism, appear to stimulate these expenditures even in a multivariate analysis that takes account of many other forces, including the changes that might explain some of the optimism. And the effect of initial assets proves to be in two different directions for different parts of the sample, distinguished in this chapter by whether or not they own a home.

Appendix A

A Description of Certain Technical
Features of the 1960-62 Survey

In this appendix certain aspects of the design of the questionnaire and the sample and the procedures for interviewing and editing in the 1960-62 panel survey are described.[1] The technical features selected for discussion are those which (1) add background information to one of the panel studies, (2) throw light upon possible sources of measurement error, or (3) reveal some of the promise- and problems- of repeated interviews with families.

Questionnaire Design

We shall comment here upon some of the questions used to obtain information about specific assets and transactions, consumer optimism, fulfillment of financial anticipations and buying plans, and income and income change.

Liquid Asset Holdings

The consumer saving measure utilized in Chapter 5 was built up from answers to a series of questions in which the respondent provided information about specific assets and transactions. Most of these questions were contained in Schedule H of the 1960 and 1962 Surveys of Consumer Finances (reproduced in this appendix).

Questions H19 through H21 in the 1962 survey were designed to elicit from the respondent "second thoughts" about his liquid asset holdings. Each respondent had been asked early in 1960 what dollar amounts he then held in checking and saving accounts and in U. S.

---

[1] This appendix is by no means complete nor even comprehensive in the areas selected for discussion. The footnotes in this appendix list references that we recommend to the reader who wishes to pursue these matters more fully.

government bonds. In 1962 the same series of questions was repeated, and after the respondent answered them he was given an envelope that contained a record of the amounts he had reported early in 1960. He was then asked whether the difference between the amounts of each component of liquid assets he reported early in 1962 and the amounts he had reported early in 1960 seemed "right" to him. The purpose of this question was to encourage the respondent to consider carefully whether the changes (flow) in each asset type over the two-year period seemed reasonably accurate and to give him an opportunity to revise his answers if he felt such revision was needed. In response to this "second thoughts" question, a small number of respondents made changes in the amounts of liquid assets they reported.

Transactions in Corporate Stocks

In questions H11 through H14 in the 1962 survey the respondent was asked about his transactions in corporate stocks over the past two years. An estimate of saving or dissaving over two years in the form of corporate stocks was prepared from his responses. The questions were designed to allow the respondent to distinguish in his answers between money put in or taken out and capital gains (or losses). Estimates of saving were prepared for respondents from the first not the second item. Thus, for respondents who were able to make these distinctions the saving measure is "cleansed" of capital gains or losses.

Index of Optimism

From the answers to questions in Schedule A, we developed the "Index of Optimism" and calculated its changes. The questions in this schedule were asked in each interview (but are reproduced here only from the 1960 survey). Chapter 2 is based upon a comparison of these answers of the respondent over the three interviews.

Fulfillment of Financial Anticipations and Buying Plans

By comparing two interviews obtained from the same respondent at different times, we obtained information on changes in response to specific questions, e.g., the respondent's anticipations about prices or about business conditions.

By comparing the answer given in one year to question A3 ("Now looking ahead, do you think you people will be better off...worse off... about the same...") to the answer given in the following year to question A1 ("Would you say that you...are better off or worse off..."), we prepared the variable called "fulfillment of financial anticipations."

The variable "fulfillment of buying plans" was prepared in a similar manner. Responses given in one interview to questions about buying plans were compared to responses given in the following interview to questions about purchases.[2] Note that we did not ask respondents whether they fulfilled their buying plans or not.

Income and Income Change

A number of important variables were constructed from answers to questions about occupation and income. The series of questions dealing with income components in Schedule G in 1960, is of special interest. Respondents were asked in detail about wages and salaries, property income, and transfer receipts of various kinds. The total income of the spending unit was calculated from the answers to these questions. Respondents were also asked questions designed to discover which member of the spending unit received what income. The variables for the study of types of income change reported in Chapter 3 were prepared from the answers to these questions about components of income, about recipients of income, and from additional questions about the number of weeks worked by the head of the spending unit.

Sample Design

The sample of spending units drawn for the 1960 Survey of Consumer Finances contained all the units in the 1960-62 panel study

[2]These questions are scattered through several schedules and are not reproduced here. The complete questionnaires are reproduced in the Survey of Consumer Finances monographs for 1960, 1961, and 1962, published by the Survey Research Center, Ann Arbor, Michigan.

(and other units which were not reinterviewed in later years). The 2972 respondents interviewed in 1960 lived in dwelling units selected in a multistage, stratified probability sample.[3] Early in 1961 we tried to reinterview about half of the 1960 sample (1520 respondents) and were able to do so in 1434 cases. Efforts made early in 1962 to re-interview all of the previous year's respondents were successful in 1059 cases. These 1059 cases, interviewed three times, make up the panel of spending units for whom we report findings here.

Sampling Discrepancies

The design of the 1960 sample differed in an important way from many prior surveys. Many of these surveys deliberately over-sampled high rent (or high house value) areas. This was not true of the 1960 sample. In selecting reinterviews, however, higher rates were applied to those with higher income, higher assets, and higher educational attainment. Further, as we did not attempt to follow movers nor attempt to introduce new respondents into the panel, the panel contained a larger proportion of homeowners and a larger pro-portion of older people than the population as a whole. We did not introduce weights to "correct" for these discrepancies because the purpose of our research was to look for relationships, not to esti-mate averages or to prepare frequency distributions. We do not wish to minimize the extent of these discrepancies. In order to reveal them more clearly, we have prepared some special tabulations to be presented in Appendix B.

It is, as a matter of fact, advantageous to have high proportions of high income and high asset consumers for certain purposes. For example, these concentrations tend to reduce the variance of the dependent variables in these ranges. The requirements of our statistical model are thus better met.

Interviewing Procedures

It is often difficult in panel surveys to maintain contact with panel members. Some of the respondents who have moved can be

---

[3]See Leslie Kish, "Selections of the Sample," in Leon Festinger and Daniel Katz (eds.) *Research Methods in the Behavioral Sciences* (New York: Dryden Press, 1953), pp. 175-239.

found only with much effort and expense. It is also time-consuming and expensive to supplement the sample with replacements for panel members who have died. Neither of these problems was encountered in the 1960-62 panel since we did not follow movers nor attempt to introduce fresh blood into the panel.

The interviewers were instructed to talk to the same respondent in each interview and were successful in doing so in almost all cases.

A discussion of interviewing theory and practice is contained in Robert L. Kahn and Charles F. Cannell, *The Dynamics of Interviewing: Theory, Techniques, and Cases,* (New York: John Wiley and Sons, 1957).

Editing Procedures

In the editing process, each completed questionnaire is checked for consistency and completeness. The editor is also required to make a number of calculations using information recorded on the questionnaire to prepare it for coding. Several editorial operations performed on the 1960-62 panel data are noted below.

1. The most intricate and important task required of the questionnaire editor in this survey was to assemble and to total the two-year saving variable. The editors were equipped with a large sheet containing spaces for asset and debt entries very much like a balance sheet of the consumer. The editor spread out the three questionnaires of the individual family and selected information from the various questions on assets, debts, and transactions. In the case of numbers pertaining to the stock of an asset, the editor subtracted the 1962 value from the 1960 value. In the case of the numbers pertaining to transactions, the editor added the value to the change in stock value after paying due attention to sign. Many editors reported after reviewing the three questionnaires that they felt they knew a good deal about the varying fortunes of individual families. The potential of panel surveys was most richly suggested at this stage.

2. After interviewing in the 1962 was underway, a deficiency in question design was discovered. In questions H24a through H24e, the respondent was asked about dollar

holdings of state and local government bonds, corporate bonds, other real estate, and so forth. If he reported nonzero amounts, he was then asked how much these amounts differed from his holdings two years earlier. (This follow-up question was asked because no information had been obtained on these items in the 1960 survey.) In a few cases (20), it was not clear whether the difference the respondent reported was positive or negative. These ambiguities resulted from improper question design rather than from faulty interviewing technique.

When the editors discovered an interview in which the direction of change was not indicated, it was returned to the interviewer with the request that he ask the respondent whether the answer represented an increase or a decrease.

Interview _____Number	FACE SHEET **A**	Sample Book Number_____

Survey Research Center
University of Michigan
Project 688
January-February 1960

	Place Sample
	_____Codes Split_____

OFFICE USE ONLY

1960 SURVEY OF CONSUMER FINANCES

Interviewer_____   Interview No._____   Date_____

INFORMATION ABOUT THE DWELLING UNIT:

1. First I'd like to know how many people 18 years and over live here?

(LIST IN SAME ORDER ON ALL FACE SHEETS FOR THIS DWELLING UNIT)

	2 Relation to Head	3 Family Unit Number	4 Sex	5 Age	6 Does he (she) usually receive $15 or more per week from any sources?	7 (IF YES) Does he (she) keep his finances separate?	8 (IF YES) Does he (she) contribute less than one-half of his income?*	9 Spend- ing Unit Number	10 Indicate Respond- ent by Check.
A	Head of DU	1			-------------	------------	------------	1	
B									
C									
D									
E									
F									
G									

11. Do any other adults live here, like roomers, servants or others? /Yes/ /No/

    (IF YES: LIST ABOVE)

(ASK ABOUT SU INTERVIEWED)

12. Do you (SU covered by this interview) have any children under 18 living here?

    (IF   13. How many?_____
    YES)
          14. How old are they?_____

* IF HE (SHE) CONTRIBUTED LESS THAN ONE-HALF, HE (SHE) IS A SEPARATE SPENDING
UNIT. IF NO, HE (SHE) IS NOT A SEPARATE SPENDING UNIT. THE MAIN SPENDING
UNIT SHOULD BE NUMBERED "1". PLEASE NUMBER ALL SPENDING UNITS.

SCHEDULE A: GENERAL ECONOMIC ATTITUDES

A1. We are interested in how people are getting along financially these days.
Would you say that you and your family are better off or worse off financially than you were a year ago?

/Better now/   /Same/   /Worse now/   /Uncertain/

A1a. Why is that?_____

_____

_____

A2. Are you people making as much money now as you were a year ago, or more,
or less?

/More now/   /About the same/   /Less now/

A2a. How is that?_____

_____

_____

A3. Now looking ahead - do you think that a year from now you people will be
better off financially, or worse off, or just about the same as now?

/Better/   /Same/   /Worse/   /Uncertain/

A4. Do you think people around here have any worries about how they'll get
along in the next year or so?· I'm speaking of people like yourself and
your friends._____

(IF YES) A4a.   What kinds of things do you or they worry about?

_____

_____

A5. Now speaking of prices in general, I mean the prices of the things you buy -
do you think they will go up in the next year or go down, or stay where they
are now?_____

A5a. Why will they do that?_____

_____

A6. Would you say that these (...rising prices; falling prices; unchanged
prices..) would be to the good, or to the bad, or what?

_____

A6a. Why do you feel that way?_____

_____

A7. Looking further ahead - do you expect that, say, about five years from now
prices of the things you buy will be higher than they are at present, lower,
or just about the same?

_____

_____

(IF DON'T   A7a. On what does it depend in your opinion?
KNOW OR
DEPENDS)   _____

_____

A8. Now, turning to business conditions in the country as a whole - Do you think
that during the next twelve months we'll have good times financially, or bad
times, or what?

/Good times/   /Good, with qualifications/   /Pro-con/

/Bad, with qualifications/   /Bad times/   /Uncertain/

A8a. Why do you think that?_____

_____

A9. Would you say that at present, business conditions are better or worse than
they were a year ago?

/Better now/   /About the same/   /Worse now/

COMMENT (IF NECESSARY):_____

A10. And how about a year from now, do you expect that in the country as a whole
business conditions will be better or worse than they are at present, or just
about the same?

/Better a year from now/   /About the same/   /Worse a year from now/

COMMENT (IF NECESSARY):_____

A11. Looking ahead, which would you say is more likely - that in the country as a
whole we'll have continuous good times during the next five years or so, or
that we will have periods of widespread unemployment or depression, or what?

_____

_____

(IF DON'T   A11a. On what does it depend in your opinion?_____
KNOW OR
DEPENDS)   _____

_____

SCHEDULE G: OCCUPATION AND INCOME

G1. What is (HEAD'S) occupation? (What sort of work does HEAD do?)_____

_____

(IF UNDERLINED UNEMPLOYED   G1a. What kind of work does (did) (HEAD) do when working?
OR RETIRED)

_____

G2. What kind of business is that in?_____

G3. Does (did) (HEAD) work for himself or someone else or what?_____

_____

(IF SELF-   G3a. Does (HEAD) regularly employ people other than himself?
EMPLOYED)   /Yes/ /No/

G4. Is head employed now (working now)?_____

G5. In 1959, how many weeks did (HEAD) work full time, including paid vacations and
     paid sick leave? _____

(IF 49
WEEKS   G6. Now about the_____weeks (HEAD) didn't work full time, was
OR LESS)   (HEAD) working part time, looking for work, ill or disabled,
                  on unpaid vacation, or what?

                       Reason   Number of Weeks

                  _____   _____

                  _____   _____

                  _____   _____

                  _____   _____

(ASK ABOUT EACH OTHER ADULT IN THE SPENDING UNIT)

(ENTER EACH OTHER ADULT HERE)———→			
G7. What is his (her) occupation? (What sort of work does he (she) usually do? (IF APPROPRIATE)			
G8. What kind of business is that in?			
G9. Does he (she) usually work for himself or someone else or what?	/Self/ /Someone Else/	/Self/ /Someone Else/	/Self/ /Someone Else/

(IF
FARMER)

G10. Did you get any soil bank payments or commodity credit loans in 1959?

/Soil bank/   /Commodity credit/   /Both/   /Neither/

G11. What were your total receipts from farming in 1959,
including these? $_____ A

G12. What were your total operating expenses, not counting
living expenses or income taxes? $_____ B

G13. That left you a net income from farming of_____ (A-B),
is that right? $_____ C

G14. Did your expenses include any investments in things
that will last for a while, like tractor, trucks,
equipment or buildings?   /Yes/ /No/

(IF YES) G15. How much went for things like that? $_____ D

G16. How much is the livestock and equipment that you own on this farm worth?
                                                              (SHOW CARD)
A /under $500/   B /$500-999/   C /$1000-4999/

D /$5000-9999/   E /$10,000-24,999/   F /$25,000 & over/

(ASK EVERYONE)

G17. Did you (R and SU) own a business any time in 1959, or did you have a financial
interest in any business enterprise?   /Yes/   /No/

(IF NO, SKIP TO PAGE 16)

(IF
YES)

G18. What sort of business is it?_____

G19. Are you the sole owner, or is it a partnership, or what?_____

G20. Is it a corporation or an unincorporated business or do you have
an interest in both kinds?

/Corporation/   (IF CORPORATION ONLY, SKIP TO PAGE 16)

/Unincorporated Business/

/Both Kinds/   (CONTINUE ON NEXT PAGE)

/Don't Know/

(ASK THIS PAGE FOR ALL UNINCORPORATED BUSINESSES (R AND SU'S SHARE)

G21. Did your business make a profit or a loss in 1959?_____

(IF PROFIT   G22. Did you (or your wife) take anything out of the business as salary,
OR BROKE   living expenses, or profit in 1959? /Yes/ /No/
EVEN)

            (IF YES) G23. How much did you take out in 1959? $_____A

        G24. In addition, did you leave any profit in the
            business? /Yes/ /No/

            (IF YES) G25. How much did you leave in, I mean
                     profits before deducting income
                     taxes? $_____B

        G26. Then if we add that in, your share of the total
            income from the business in 1959 before deducting
            income taxes was (A+B), is that about right? $_____C

(IF   G27. How much was your loss in 1959? $_____D
LOSS)
        G28. Did you (or your wife) take anything out of the
            business as salary or living expenses in 1959? /Yes/ /No/

            (IF YES) G29. How much did you take out in 1959? $_____E

                    G30. If you had left that money in the
                         business, how much profit or loss
                         would the business have shown? $_____F

G31. Does the business owe any money for business improvements, new equipment, new
buildings, and things like that? /Yes/ /No/

G32. Did you pay off any money in 1959 that you owed on things like that? /Yes/ /No/

     (IF   G33. Some people think of money used to pay off business debts as part
     YES)   of the expenses of their business and some think of it as profit
                   used to increase the value of their business. Did you count this
                   money you paid off in 1959 as a business expense or as part of
                   profit? /Business expense/ /Profit/

                 (IF BUSINESS   G34. How much did you reduce your
                 EXPENSE)   business debt during 1959? $_____

G35. How much is your share of the business worth? (SHOW CARD)

    A /less than $500/   B /$500-999/   C /$1000-4999/

    D /$5000-9999/   E /$10,000-24,999/   F /$25,000 & over/

In this survey all over the country we are trying to get an accurate picture of people's financial situation. One thing we need to know is the income of all the people we interview.

(ASK EVERYONE)

G36. How much did you (HEAD) receive from wages and salaries in 1959, that is, before deductions for taxes or anything? $_____

G37. In addition to this, did you have any income from bonuses, overtime, and commissions? /Yes/ /No/

(IF YES) G38. How much was that? $_____

G39. Did you receive any (other) income from:

(IF "YES" TO ANY ITEM)
How much was your income from (SOURCE) after allowing for expenses?
(ENTER AMOUNT AT RIGHT)

a) professional practice $_____

b) a trade $_____

c) farming or market gardening $_____

d) roomers and boarders $_____

e) any other self-employment $_____

f) rent $_____

G40. How about:

a) interest............................ $_____

b) dividends........................... $_____

c) trust fund or royalties............. $_____

d) veteran's pension, veteran's school allotment, serviceman's family allotment.......................... $_____

e) unemployment compensation........... $_____

f) Social Security..................... $_____

g) other retirement pay, pensions, annuities.......................... $_____

h) alimony, regular contributions from family........................ $_____

i) public welfare, other government aid...................... $_____

NOTE TO INTERVIEWER:
LEAVE NO BLANK SPACES,
ENTER ZERO IF NONE.

TOTAL $_____

(Carry forward to top of next page)

(Total from previous page) $_____

Now about the income of other members of the family (SU) -

(INCOME
OF WIFE)

G41. Did your wife have any income during the year?
/Yes/ /No/

(IF   G42. Was it from wages, salary, a business
YES)   or what?
         G43. How much did she receive?

SOURCE (G42)			
AMOUNT (G43)	$	$	$

= $_____

(IF YES   G44. How many weeks did she
TO G41)   work full time?

_____

         G45. How many weeks did she
                work part time?

_____

(INCOME
OF
OTHER
MEMBERS
OF SU)

G46. Did_____(MENTION OTHER MEMBERS OF SU)
     have any income? /Yes/   /No/

(IF   G47. Who?
YES)   G48. Was it from wages, salary, a business
                or what?
         G49. How much was it?

WHO (G47)			
SOURCE (G48)			
AMOUNT (G49)	$	$	$

= $_____

(IF BUSINESS INCOME from G26 or G30, ENTER IT HERE.....(BUSINESS) $_____
(IF FARM INCOME from G13, ENTER IT HERE....................(FARM) $_____

G50. Adding everything up, I get.....................(SU TOTAL) $_____
     for the total of yourself (and your wife and children)
     for the year. Is that about right?

G51. Is this amount (SU Total) larger or smaller than what you
     people received the year before, in 1958, or just the same?

_____

G52. What would you say your total income was in 1958, you and
     others in SU? $_____

SCHEDULE H: OTHER ASSETS

H1.   Do you (R and SU) carry life insurance?   /Yes/   /No/

> (IF
> YES)
>
> H2.   How much did you (entire SU) put into life insurance payments
> (premiums) in 1959?
>
> $_____

H3.   Did you (R and SU) take out any new policies during 1959?   /Yes/   /No/

H4.   Do you (R and SU) own any common or preferred stock in a corporation, including
companies you have worked for?   /Yes/   /No/

H5.   Do you (R and SU) own shares in a mutual fund or investment club?   /Yes/   /No/

> (IF OWNS
> STOCK,
> SHARES
> IN MUTUAL
> FUND, ETC.)
>
> H6.   Is it stock or shares that are sold to the general public, or stock
> in a privately held corporation?
> /Sold to general public/   /Privately held/   /Both/   /Uncertain/
>
> H7.   Speaking now only of stock sold to the general public, in how many
> different corporations do you own stock?
>
> _____
>
> H8.   About how much are these stocks (sold to the general public) worth?
> (SHOW CARD)
>
> A /less than $500/   B /$500-999/   C /$1000-4999/
>
> D /$5000-9999/   E /$10,000-24,999/   F /$25,000 & over/

H9.   Do you own any real estate (aside from your own home) such as a house or cottage,
or an apartment house, farm, commercial or rental property?
/Yes/   /No/

> (IF
> YES)
>
> H10.   What kind of property is it?_____
>
> H11.   How much would you say the property is worth altogether?
> (SHOW CARD)
>
> A /less than $500/   B /$500-999/   C /$1000-4999/
>
> D /$5000-9999/   E /$10,000-24,999/   F /$25,000 & over/

Most of us have debts, but we also have savings, and that's what this final part is about.

(IF
UNINCORPORATED
BUSINESSMAN)

H12. Do you keep the bonds and bank accounts of the business separate from your personal funds?

/Separate/   /Not separate/

(IF SEPARATE)   H12a. Then lets talk about your personal funds only.

(IF NOT
SEPARATE)   H12b. Then lets talk about your combined business and personal funds.

(GO TO NEXT PAGE)

H13. Do you or your wife (husband) have any regular government war bonds, or savings bonds, or defense bonds? /Yes/ /No/

   (IF YES. H14. How much are they worth (face value)? $_____

H15. How about other members of your family (SU), do they have any such bonds, or are there any bonds you hold for your children? /Yes/ /No/

   (IF YES) H16. How much are they worth (face value)? $_____

Savings accounts are another frequent form in which savings and reserve funds are kept. We know that it is not easy to give accurate answers to these questions, so we would appreciate it if you would look up bank-books or other records.

H17. Do you or your wife (husband) have any savings accounts?

   /Yes/ /No/

   (IF YES)   H18. Are these accounts with banks, savings and loan associations, credit unions, or several of these?

   /Bank/   /Savings and Loan Assn./   /Credit Union/

   (MAKE 2 OR 3 CHECK MARKS, IF NECESSARY)

   H19. How much money do you have in all these accounts? $_____

H20. How about other members of your family (SU), do any of them have savings accounts; including accounts of your children? /Yes/ /No/

   (IF YES)   H21. Are these accounts with banks, savings and loan associations, credit unions, or several of these?

   /Bank/   /Savings and Loan Assn./   /Credit Union/

   H22. How much money is in these savings accounts? $_____

                                                     (subtotal) $_____

                    (CARRY SUBTOTAL FORWARD TO TOP OF NEXT PAGE)

(Subtotal from previous page) $_____

H23. Finally, checking accounts in banks - do you or anyone in
     your family (SU) have any checking accounts? /Yes/ /No/

     (IF YES) H24. How much money is in the checking accounts? $_____

H25. Adding up what you and your family (SU) have in government
     bonds, savings and checking accounts, you have... ....$_____
     is that right?

H26. How about a year ago altogether did you and your family (SU)
     have more or less in bonds and bank accounts at that time?

     /More a year ago/   /Same/   /Less a year ago/

H27. What is your best estimate about how large these savings
     were a year ago,

     first, in government bonds $_____

     in savings accounts $_____

     in checking accounts $_____

INTERVIEWER:
_____

H28. Were any records looked up in bonds, savings or checking account questions?

      /Yes/ /No/

The University of Michigan
Survey Research Center
Project 699   1961 SURVEY OF CONSUMER FINANCES
January-February 1961

Re-interview

Sample Book No._____

Place Codes_____

1960 Int. No._____
Do not write in above spaces

1. Interviewer's Name_____

2. Interview Number_____   2a. Date_____

COPY LISTING BOX INFORMATION FROM "WORK" LISTING BOX ON INFORMATION SHEET:
LIST ALL PERSONS 18 YEARS OF AGE AND OVER WHO RESIDE AT THIS DWELLING UNIT.

3	4	5	6	7	8	9	10	11	12
Relationship to Head	Family Unit Number	Sex	Age	Does he(she) usually receive $15 or more per wk. from any source?	(IF YES) Does he(she) keep his finances separate?	(IF YES) Does he(she) contribute less than one-half of his income?*	Spending Unit Number	Indicate R by Check (✓)	Did he (she) live here a year ago?
Head of DU	1			----------	----------	----------	1		

(INTERVIEW HEAD OF DU (SU #1), MAKE OUT BLUE COVER SHEET AND TAKE SEPARATE INTERVIEW WITH HEAD
OF EACH SECONDARY SPENDING UNIT AT THIS DWELLING UNIT.)

13. Do you (SU covered by this interview) have any children under 18 living here?   NO
                                                                            YES

    13a. How many?_____

    13b. How old are they?_____

* IF HE(SHE) IS "YES" TO Q.7, 8, and 9, HE (SHE) IS A SEPARATE SPENDING UNIT. IF "NO" TO
ANY ONE OF THEM, HE (SHE) IS NOT A SEPARATE SPENDING UNIT. THE MAIN SPENDING UNIT SHOULD
BE NUMBERED "1". PLEASE NUMBER ALL SPENDING UNITS.

(IF WORKING NOW, UNEMPLOYED, LAID-OFF, OR RETIRED)

G2. What is your (HEAD) occupation? What sort of work do (did) you do?

_____

G3. What kind of business is (was) that in?_____

G4. Do (did) you (HEAD) work for yourself or someone else, or what?_____

(IF   G5. Do you (HEAD) regularly employ people
SELF)   other than yourself?   YES   NO

             G6. How long have you (HEAD) been working for yourself?

             _____

             (IF LESS G7. How many different full-time jobs have you
             THAN 15   had since the World War ended in 1945?
             YEARS)

             _____

(IF   G8. How long have you (HEAD) been with your present employer?
SOMEONE
ELSE)   _____

             (IF LESS G9. How many different full-time jobs have you had
             THAN 15   since the World War ended in 1945?
             YEARS)

             _____

G10. What did you do on your first full-time regular job?_____

_____

G11. When was that?_____

G12. What did you earn during your first year at that?

      $_____ per_____(month, week, year)

G13. Considering what you looked forward to, would you say that you have made good
progress, or that you are not quite satisfied with your progress?

_____

_____

G14. You've told us what your present position is and what you did on your first full-time regular job--Did you ever work along a different line?

| NO |

| YES |

G14a. Tell me about it? _____

_____

G15. When people look back at their job history, often one or two important things stand out; did something happen with you that affected your way of working and making money?

| NO |

| YES |

G16. What was that? _____

G17. When was that? _____

(CHECK BACK SEVERAL QUESTIONS TO Q.G11, PAGE 13, DATE OF FIRST FULL TIME REGULAR JOB)

(If ☐   Before 1920..............SKIP TO Q.G18 AND CONTINUE SEQUENCE

(CHECK " ☐   1920-27................. " " Q.G19 "   "   "
BOX)   " ☐   1928-39................. " " Q.G20 "   "   "

     " ☐   1940-45................. " " Q.G21 "   "   "
     " ☐   1946.................... " " Q.G22 "   "   "
     " ☐   1947-55................. " " Q.G23 "   "   "

     " ☐   1956-60................. " " Q.G25 "   "   "

G18. Thinking back to the time after the first World War, how much did you make around 1920? $_____ per_____ [month / week / year]

G19. Thinking back to the time before the depression hit, how much did you make around 1928? $_____ per_____ [month / week / year]

G20. Thinking back to the years just before World War II, how much did you make around 1940? $_____ per_____ [month / week / year]

G21. Thinking back to the period of the Second World War, 1941-46, we're interested in whether the war made a difference in how much you earned--because of the war do you think you earned more or less during that period than you would have, or about the same? _____

G22. Thinking back to the time after things settled down following World War II, how much did you make around 1947? $_____ per_____ [month / week / year]

G23. About how much did you make 5 years ago, in 1955? $_____ per_____ [month / week / year]

(CHECK BACK TO G11, PAGE 13, AGAIN:)

(IF G11. | G24. Has your income been quite steady during the last ten years or so,
IS BEFORE | or has it been going up, or down, or changing from time to time?
1950)
_____

G24a. Why is that?_____

_____

(IF G11. | G25. Since you began working full-time, has your income been going
IS 1950- | up, or down, or changing from time to time?
1960)
_____

G25a. Why is that?_____

_____

(ASK EVERYONE

G26. Was there ever a time when (your wife or) other family members had income and
     contributed to family finances?   [NO]--(SKIP TO INSTRUCTIONS FOR Q.G31, PAGE 16)

                                        [YES]
                                                      OTHERS (FILL IN BELOW)

G27. Who was it?   [WIFE]   _____ _____

G28. When was that?   _____ _____ _____

G29. Was this income from earnings?   _____ _____ _____

G30. During the last ten years did most of your family income come from (your
     wife or) other family members, or did most of it come from your earnings,
     or what?
     _____

G31. Do you think your wife will work in the future? [YES] [NO]

G32. Since you (HEAD) got your first regular job, what other states have you lived in (not including your experience while in military service)?

NONE, ONLY THIS STATE	OTHERS (LIST→)

(IF NONE) G33. Since your first regular job, have you ever lived more than 100 miles from here?

G34. Have you (HEAD) ever been unemployed or laid-off? [NO] -- (SKIP TO Q.H1, PAGE 17)

[YES]

G35. Some people are out of work for a time every year, others are unemployed every few years, and for still others unemployment is quite unusual. How has it been in your case?

Schedule J: FINANCIAL EXPERIENCE AND EXPECTATIONS

(G.J1-J3 OMITTED FROM THIS SCHEDULE)

J4.   Did anything ever happen that cost you a good deal of money, such as an accident, prolonged illness, fire, business loss, or the like?

_____

(IF   J5.   When was that?_____
YES)
      J6.   What happened?_____

      J7.   How did you take care of it financially?_____

      _____

J8.   Suppose your family had to pay a very large medical bill equal to about two months income and not covered by insurance. How would you handle such a major medical expense?

_____

J9.   Do you people have any savings, investments, or reserve funds?

                                               NO -- (SKIP TO Q.J17,P.23)

(IF   YES
YES) J10. How do you feel about the amount you now have of these--is it far too little, fairly satisfactory, fully adequate, or what?

      _____

      J11. Was there any time during the past ten years or so when you people had more savings, investments, or reserve funds than you have now?

            NO --(SKIP TO Q.J13, PAGE 23)

            YES

            J12. How is it that you now have less?_____

            _____

      (CONTINUE WITH Q.J13 ON NEXT PAGE)

J13. Do you have any plans for large expenditures for which you would
      use your savings or reserve funds? [NO]

                                        [YES]
      J14. What are they?_____

      J15. When would that be?_____

            (IF NOT   J16. Do you think you will have to spend
            MENTIONED)   large amounts for schooling or educa-
                                tion of your children?

                                _____

(SKIP TO Q.J20)

(IF NO TO Q.J9, PAGE 22)

J17. Was there any time during the past ten years or so when you people had some
      savings, investments or reserve funds ?

            [NO] -- SKIP TO Q.J25, PAGE 24)

            [YES]
      J18. When was that?_____

      J19. How is it that you now have less?_____

            _____

J20. In your case what are the main purposes of saving?_____

      _____

      J20a. Anything else?_____

J21.   Altogether, would you say that during the past twelve months you people have
       increased your savings or reserves, or did you use up some of them, or did
       you break even?

   (IF   J22.   In what form are these additional savings or reserves?
   SAVED)

                          J22a. Anything else?_____

   (IF   J23.   In what form were these savings or reserves that you used?
   DECREASED
   SAVINGS
   OR
   RESERVES)   J24.   What did you use the money for?_____

J25.   Have you ever owned a house of your own? | NO | -- (SKIP TO Q.J29)

                                  | YES |

J26. When did you first own a house of your own?_____

J27. Have you owned more than one? | YES | | NO |

J28. While you owned this (these) house(s), would you say that the value increased
     greatly, a little bit, or not at all?

J29.   Have you ever benefited from other real estate, stocks, a business or anything
       which has increased a great deal in value?

J30. Have you (or your wife) ever inherited any money or property?

> NO
>
> YES
>
>> J31. When was that?_____
>>
>> J32. What was it worth?_____

J33. What about large gifts of money or property from parents or relatives, have you ever gotten anything like that?

> NO
>
> YES
>
>> J34. When was that?_____
>>
>> J35. What was it worth?_____

(IF
YES TO
Q.J30 OR
Q.J33)

> J36. Considering your total family assets or reserve funds now -- did most of them come from inheritance or gifts, or did you save most of them out of income?
>
> _____
>
> _____

(IF HEAD IS NOT RETIRED AND NOT A HOUSEWIFE)

J37. Turning to the future; some people change jobs occasionally. Do you think you will have a different job in a few years, or will you almost certainly keep your present job, or what?

> DIFFERENT JOB   PRESENT JOB   OTHER

J38. Why do you think so?_____

_____

J39. During the next ten years or so, do you think your earnings will rise gradually, go up and down from year to year, or fall, or what?

_____

J40. In some lines of work the top income is reached when one is fairly young, in other lines close to retirement. How is it in your line of work?

_____

J41. What would a person make a year at that time (top income)? $_____

J42. How about you, what might be the highest (yearly) income you think you will earn before you retire?

            $_____

J43. About when do you think you will reach that?_____

(IF HEAD IS <u>EITHER</u> <u>RETIRED</u>, A <u>HOUSEWIFE</u>, OR <u>UNDER</u> 35 YEARS OLD, SKIP TO SCHEDULE K, P.27)

(IF HEAD IS NEITHER RETIRED NOR HOUSEWIFE, AND IS 35 OR MORE YEARS OLD)

J44. Could you tell me when you think you will retire from the work you now do, I mean in how many years?

_____

J45. How will you manage financially after your retirement? Tell me your plans.

_____

_____

_____

(IF <u>NOT</u>   J46. Will you be doing any work for pay?_____
CLEAR)

_____

J47. Will you get social security?_____

(IF   J48. What monthly or yearly income can you expect from this?
YES)
         $_____ per_____(year, month)

J49. Apart from social security, some people have retirement or pension plans, or annuities -- do you have any of these?

_____

(IF   J50. What monthly or yearly income can you expect from this?
YES)
         $_____ per_____(year, month)

J51. Will you have a home of your own, when you retire?

_____

(IF   J52. Will it be fully paid for? | YES | | NO |
YES)

The University of Michigan
Survey Research Center   1962 SURVEY OF CONSUMER FINANCES
Project 707
January-February 1962

A

Sample Book No._____

Place Codes_____

_____

Do **not** write in above spaces

1. Interviewer's Name_____

2. Your Int. No. _____   2a. Date_____

(COPY LISTING BOX INFORMATION FROM "WORK" LISTING BOX ON THE 1962 INFORMATION SHEET:
LIST ALL PERSONS 18 YEARS OF AGE AND OVER WHO RESIDE AT THIS <u>DWELLING UNIT</u>.)

a. Relationship to Head	b. Family Unit Number	c. Sex	d. Age	e. Does he(she) usually re-ceive $15 or more per wk. from any source?	f. (IF <u>YES</u>) Does he(she) keep his fi-nances sepa-rate?	g. (IF <u>YES</u>) Does he(she) contribute less than one-half of his income?*	h. Spend-ing Unit Number	i. Indi-cate R by Check (✓)	j. Did he (she) live here in '60 '61
Head of DU	1			-----------	-----------	-----------	1		

(INTERVIEW HEAD OF DU (SU #1). MAKE OUT BLUE COVER SHEET, AND TAKE SEPARATE INTERVIEW
WITH HEAD OF EACH SECONDARY SPENDING UNIT AT THIS DWELLING UNIT.)

3. Do you (SU covered by this interview) have any children under 18 living here?   [No]

[Yes]

    3a. How many?_____

    3b. How old are they?_____

*(IF HE(SHE) IS "YES" IN COLS. e, f, <u>and</u> g, HE(SHE) IS A SEPARATE SPENDING UNIT. IF
"NO" TO ANY ONE OF THEM, HE(SHE) IS <u>NOT</u> A SEPARATE SPENDING UNIT. THE MAIN SPENDING
UNIT SHOULD BE NUMBERED "1". PLEASE NUMBER ALL SPENDING UNITS.)

Schedule H: OTHER ASSETS AND SAVINGS

H1. Do you (R and SU) carry life insurance? | No |
                                               | Yes |

> H1a. How much did you (entire SU) put into life insurance payments (premiums)
>   in 1961? $_____

H2. Do you (R and SU) owe any money on a policy loan from a life insurance company?
    | No | | Yes |

> H2a. How much do you owe? $_____

H3. Did you (R and SU) take out any new policies during 1961? | Yes | | No |

H4. Do you (R and SU) own any common or preferred stock in a corporation, including
    companies you have worked for, or own stock through an investment club, or own
    shares of a mutual fund?   (✓ THE APPROPRIATE BOXES)

☐ (OWN CORPORATE STOCK DIRECTLY--INCLUDING COMPANIES WORKED FOR)
☐ (OWN STOCK THROUGH AN INVESTMENT CLUB)   (GO TO
☐ (OWN SHARES OF A MUTUAL FUND(S))   Q. H6)
☐ (OWN NO STOCKS OR SHARES)

> H5. Two years ago did you own any stocks or shares in a corporation or
>   mutual fund? | No |--(SKIP TO P. 23, Q. H15)
> | Yes |
>
> > H5a. Altogether what was the total value in stocks or shares that
> >   you (entire SU) held two years ago? $_____
> >   (SKIP TO PAGE 23, Q. H15)

(IF OWNS STOCK OR MUTUAL FUND SHARES)

> H6. Is it stock that is sold to the general public, or stock in a privately
>   held corporation?
> | Sold to general public | | Privately held | | Both | | D.K. |
>
> | | Publicly Traded | Privately Held |
> |--|-----------------|----------------|
> | H7. How much are these stocks worth? | $_____ | $_____ |
> | H8. Do you owe any money in connection with your stock? | No |--(SKIP TO PAGE 23, Q. H11) | |
> | | Yes | | | |
> | H9. How much do you owe? | $_____ | $_____ |
> | H10. That leaves your net investment in stock . . . . | $_____ | $_____ |
> | Is that right? | Yes |--(GO TO P. 23, Q. H11) | | |
> | | No |--(CORRECT H7-H10) | | |

(IF OWNS STOCK OR MUTUAL FUND SHARES -- CONTINUED)

H11.   Stock prices change and people also put money into stocks and take money
       out. Did you put new money into stock or take money out "on balance" over
       the last two years? | Put money in | | Took money out | | Same |

       H12. How much? $_____

H13.   Altogether would you say that the net value of the stocks and shares that
       you hold today is greater or less than the net value of your holdings two
       years ago? | Greater today | | Less today | | Same |

       H14. How much would you estimate that the value has changed? $_____

(ASK EVERYONE)

H15.   Do you or others in your family (SU) have any regular government savings bonds,
       war bonds or defense bonds? | No |
                                     | Yes |

       H15a. How much do you (SU) have altogether?   (FACE VALUE) $_____

H16.   Do you or others in your family (SU) have any savings accounts in
       banks, savings or building and loan associations, or credit unions?
                                     | No |
                                     | Yes |

       H16a. How much do you (SU) have altogether in:

       Banks? . . . . | None | $_____
       Savings (Building) and Loan Associations? . . . . | None | $_____
       Credit Unions? . . . . | None | $_____

H17.   Do you or others in your family (SU) have any checking accounts at
       banks? | No |
                 | Yes |

       H17a. How much do you (SU) have in your checking account(s) now? $_____

H18.   Adding up your checking accounts, savings accounts, and savings
       bonds, I get . . . .   1962 TOTAL $_____
       Is that right? | Yes |
                         | No | --(CORRECT H15-H17a)

(BRING OUT SEALED ENVELOPE)

We're interested in finding out about changes in your savings during the last two years. I have in this envelope the information you gave us two years ago since it is hard to remember. Could we look it over now and see if the changes from 1960 seem reasonable to you?

| Yes | | No |--(ANSWER Q. H23 AND SKIP TO PAGE 25, Q. H24)

(ASK FOR EACH ITEM THE FAMILY (SU) OWNED EITHER YEAR)

(BONDS)

H19. In bonds now you have $_____(FROM H15-H15a);

      Two years ago you had $_____(FROM SEALED ENVELOPE);

      If I subtract there is $_____ _____(MORE/LESS) now.

      Does that seem right to you? | Yes | | No |--(REVISE H15, H15a, OR H19)

(SAVINGS ACCOUNTS)

H20. In savings accounts now you have $_____(FROM H16, H16a);

      Two years ago you had . . . . . $_____(FROM SEALED ENVELOPE)

      If I subtract there is . . . . . $_____ _____(MORE/LESS) now.

      Does that seem right to you? | Yes | | No |--(REVISE H16, H16a, OR H20)

(CHECKING ACCOUNTS)

H21. In checking accounts now you have $_____(FROM H17, H17a);

      Two years ago you had . . . . . . $_____(FROM SEALED ENVELOPE)

      If I subtract there is . . . . . . $_____ _____(MORE/LESS) now.

      Does that seem right to you? | Yes |

                                   | No |
┌───┐
│ H21a. How much has your checking account changed from two years ago?   │
│   │
│ $_____ _____(MORE NOW/LESS NOW)   │
└───┘

(INTERVIEWER)
┌───┐
│ H22. Were any changes or revisions made in response to H19-H21? | No | │
│ | Yes | │
│   ┌──┐   │
│   │ H22a. How did these changes come about?_____ │   │
│   │   _____│   │
│   │   _____│   │
│   │   _____│   │
│   └──┘   │
│   │
│ H23. What records did R use in answering Questions H15-H21a?   │
│ | None | _____   │
│   _____   │
└───┘

H24. Now about other kinds of investment--do you people have any . . .

    a.   other U.S. government bonds (marketable or current interest bearing)?

       ☐ YES
          1) How much? $_____
          2) How much different is this amount from 2 years ago? $_____

       ☐ NO
          3) Did you own any 2 years ago?
              [Yes]   [No]
          4) How much? $_____

    b.   state or local bonds?

       ☐ YES
          1) How much? $_____
          2) How much different is this amount from 2 years ago? $_____

       ☐ NO
          3) Did you own any 2 years ago?
              [Yes]   [No]
          4) How much? $_____

    c.   corporate bonds?

       ☐ YES
          1) How much? $_____
          2) How much different is this amount from 2 years ago? $_____

       ☐ NO
          3) Did you own any 2 years ago?
              [Yes]   [No]
          4) How much? $_____

    d.   other real estate (besides this home)?

       ☐ YES
          1) What do you own?
              _____
          2) How much is it(are they) worth? $_____
          3) How much different is this amount from 2 years ago? $_____

       ☐ NO
          4) Did you own any 2 years ago?
              [Yes]   [No]
          5) How much? $_____

    e.   mortgages or land contracts owed to you?

       ☐ YES
          1) How much are they worth? $_____
          2) How much different is this amount from 2 years ago? $_____

       ☐ NO
          3) Did you own any 2 years ago?
              [Yes]   [No]
          4) How much? $_____

(IF ANY "YES" TO H24 a-e)

H25. How about loans associated with any of these investments; do you now **owe** any
      money associated with these items? | No |
                                                  | Yes |

    H25a. Which ones? . . . . _____   _____   _____

    H25b. How much do you owe now? . $_____ $_____ $_____

    H25c. How much did you owe two
            years ago on this type
            of loan? . . . . $_____ $_____ $_____

H26. Have you inherited any money or property in the last year?

    | No |
    | Yes |

    H27. What was it worth? $_____

(IF HAS ANY SAVINGS OR INVESTMENTS)

    H28. Thinking back over what has happened to your savings, investments, and reserve
           funds in the last two years, do you feel satisfied or dissatisfied?

    _____

    H29. What do you have in mind?_____

    _____

Appendix B

Panel Mortality in the 1960-61-62 Surveys of Consumer Finances*

Two types of losses occur in any panel study: nonresponse and moving. In this appendix we shall (1) estimate losses due to these two factors and (2) study characteristics of movers and subsequent nonrespondents in order to see what effects these phenomena have on the composition of the panel. Panel studies offer a unique opportunity for studying the composition of the moving population. It is also possible to study the characteristics of those who are not successfully interviewed on a second or a third wave, who may be similar to the noninterview population in general.

The source of the data for this study is the three-year panel formed from the Surveys of Consumer Finances of 1960, 1961, and 1962. From the 1960 original sample of almost 3000, it was decided for reasons of economy to have a sample of only about 2000 in 1961 and 1962. Therefore differential selection rates were used in selecting 1960 addresses for reinterview in 1961 and 1962. A two-thirds selection rate was used for "noncriterion" addresses while "criterion" addresses were selected with certainty. A criterion address was defined as one containing a spending unit meeting any *one* of the following criteria: income of $7500 or more, total assets of $25,000 or more, or a college graduate as head. As a result of this selection procedure, there were 642 spending units interviewed in 1960 who lived at addresses not selected for reinterview in 1961. Sixty per cent of the addresses not selected in 1961 were subsequently selected for interview in 1962. There remained 273 originally interviewed spending units living at addresses which were *not* included for reinterview in either 1961 or 1962.

As a consequence of these sampling designs, we obtained three panels. The main panel of interest to us is made up of spending units interviewed three times—1960, 1961, and 1962. These spending units

*Written by Albert M. Marckwardt.

numbered 1059. A larger panel was interviewed twice 1960 and 1961 and numbered 1434 spending units. Finally a much smaller number were interviewed in 1960 and 1962. Despite the complex sample design, the findings in this study are not influenced by the nonrepresentative composition of the panels, since weights have been calculated to adjust for differential selection rates so as to re-establish the original sample proportions. These weights were used in the tabulations of this appendix only.

We are focusing here on a description of findings uncovered by simple cross-tabulations. These data are presented in tabular form in the tables accompanying this report. The three sections of this appendix deal with differential reinterview response rates, residential stability (nonmoving) rates, and the composition of the panels. Some of the highlights of this study include the following:

1. People who have been previously interviewed are somewhat more willing to grant an interview than are people who are approached the first time.

2. Reinterview response rates, in general, vary inversely with socio-economic status. However, differentials stand out less sharply in the case of the second reinterview (i.e., the third wave).

3. Residential stability (nonmoving) rates generally show the opposite pattern to that of response rates in their variation with socio-economic status. Additionally, younger spending units and those who rent are more likely to move.

4. Due to the comparative size of the moving group as compared with the noninterview group, the effects due to moving are always greater on the panel. As a result, panels tend to have an upward financial bias.

Differential Reinterview Response Rates

The 1961 reinterview response rate among units still there in 1961 was 83.3 per cent. The response rate in 1962 for those who had been interviewed in *both* 1960 and 1961 was 86.5 per cent. These figures compare with a figure of about 80 per cent which has been the response rate on recent Surveys of Consumer Finances, indicating that people who have been previously interviewed are somewhat more willing to give interviews than are people who are approached the first time. An earlier study of the five-wave panel limited to urban areas revealed similar findings.[1]

Response rates vary with education (Table B-1); the highest response rates occur among spending units headed by someone with a college degree. In general, it appears that response rates are lowest among those groups headed by persons who did not complete an academic program. Thus, looking at the 1961 response rates we find that lowest response rates in the categories "some high school," and "some college." It is interesting to note, however, an apparent reversal for the second reinterview. The response rate for those with "some high school" increases sharply. In general it will be shown that response rates for the second reinterview do not demonstrate the clear or sharp patterns found among the first time reinterviews.

Table B-2 shows that reinterview response rates are lowest among spending units having large liquid asset holdings and are highest among those with modest holdings. Once again, however, differences are small for the second time reinterview.

With respect to the income of spending units (Table B-3) those having large incomes are less likely to grant a reinterview, while those with low and modest incomes (up to $5000) are most likely to grant reinterviews. This particular differential is also found in the second reinterview.

There seems to be little difference in response rates as between homeowners and renters, as shown by Table B-4. Primary units who neither own nor rent and unrelated secondaries tend to have higher response rates than other groups, and related secondaries have generally lower response rates. The pattern of response rates with respect to duration of housing status is mixed.

With respect to response rate differentials by a classification of location of residence (Table B-5), two findings stand out: (1) response rates are lowest in the central cities of the twelve largest Standard Metropolitan Statistical Areas, and (2) they are highest in adjacent and outlying areas.

There is much variation of response rates between the various

---

[1]Marion Gross Sobel, "Panel Mortality and Panel Bias," *Journal of the American Statistical Association*, LIV (March 1959), 52-68.

occupational groups. Table B-6 shows that the white collar groups generally have the lowest response rates and the blue collar and retired groups have about average response rates, whereas the farmers and the unemployed have fairly high response rates. The generally high response rate among farmers is consistent with our earlier finding that such rates are high in adjacent and outlying areas. Similarly, the low response rate among white collar workers is in keeping with our previous findings regarding response rates among upper income and asset groups.

Very marked differences in response rates appear between age groups (Table B-7). By far the highest response rates are obtained in the age group 18-24, whereas low response rates may be observed among the age group 45-54.

Residential Stability (Nonmoving) Rates

This section presents data on differential rates of residential stability. The two final righthand columns of Tables B-1 through B-7 show the percentage of spending units interviewed in 1960 remaining unchanged at the same address in 1961 and 1962. The figures for 1962 are not broken down, as were the response rates, between those whose addresses were visited in 1961 and those whose addresses were not visited, because moving rates are not likely to be affected by the interviewer's visit. A spending unit was considered "unchanged" if the head of the spending unit did not change. Subtracting the percentages in either of the final two columns from 100 will give the percentage of spending units that either moved or changed composition. Most of these, by far, are movers.

By interview data in 1961 only 76.4 per cent of the spending units interviewed in 1960 remained unchanged at the same address. By 1962 this figure had dropped to 66.2 per cent. Table B-1 shows that spending unit heads with only grammar school education or less were most likely to remain at the same address in 1961. However, the same patterns do not hold for 1962. It was clear that in that year the most stable group were those with some high school education. In general it appears that the spending units headed by someone with a college degree are less stable residentially than other groups. Table B-2 shows that residential stability rates vary greatly with level of liquid asset holdings. There is a very smooth upward pattern in stability rates as liquid assets increase. This indicates that people with low financial reserves are the ones most likely to move, or to reconstitute. Residential stability rates show about the same pattern with respect to income (Table B-3). Low rates of residential stability are associated with low incomes and high stability rates with high incomes. In both 1961 and 1962 the lowest residential stability rates occurred in the income group $3000 to $4999; stability rates were higher at each higher income level. It is interesting to note that, in general, residential stability rates show just the opposite pattern to that of response rates in their variation with income.

Marked differences in residential stability rates occur with housing status and duration (Table B-4). Homeowners are the most stable group and renters who have recently moved in are the least stable. Primary spending units who neither own nor rent and unrelated and related secondaries are also very mobile. The magnitude of these differences is great. Whereas 90 per cent of the owners interviewed in 1960 who purchased before 1957 were at the same address in 1961, only 50 per cent of the recent renters were found to be at the same address a year later, and only 32 per cent of these renters were likely to be there two years later. Hence, any reinterview study in which movers are not followed will have a disproportionately high percentage of homeowners.

Spending units residing in suburban areas and adjacent areas tend to be the most stable (Table B-5). Mobility is greatest in the central cities of the smaller Standard Metropolitan Statistical Areas.

Residential stability rates vary greatly with differences in age (Table B-7). The figures for 1961 show that residential stability rates are very low in the 18-24 year group and rise steadily through the 55-64 group and then decreased slightly for those 65 or older. Figures for 1962 reach a maximum of residential stability in the 45-54 year group and then decline a little in the 55-64 group. Since spending unit heads are classified by their age in 1960 it is possible that some of the decline in 55-64 year group occurred because of people who turned 65 and moved as a result of retirement. These data indicate that a reinterview study at fixed addresses will be heavily weighted with older spending units. However, the low stability rates among the very young spending units is partially offset by their higher response rates.

Composition of the Panels

We noted earlier that there are two sources of loss to a panel, moving and nonresponse. We have examined some of the differentials in nonresponse rates and in residential stability (nonmoving) rates. The effects of these two sources of loss on the resulting composition in both the 1960-1961 reinterviews and the three-year panel are shown in Tables B-8 through B-14; these data are tabulated by the same classifying variables as used in Tables B-1 through B-6. The second column in Tables B-8 through B-14 is closed off with dotted lines from the losses due to moving and noninterviews. Though non-selection constitutes a loss to the unweighted panel, this particular source of loss does not affect the remaining columns of the tables since the weights used compensate for nonselection. In other words, losses from this source are not reflected in the columns reporting the composition of the succeeding panels. The most meaningful comparisons using these tables can be drawn through comparing the composition of the two panels with the 1960 sample. The basis for the differences between the panel and the full sample can be seen in the composition of the moving and noninterview losses.

Table B-8 shows that the panels differ little from the original sample with respect to distribution of educational attainment The generally higher mobility rates in the upper educational groups are offset by lower nonresponse rates. Table B-9 clearly shows an affect that we noted earlier--that the moving population is highly concentrated among those holding little liquid assets early in 1960. This phenomenon is not entirely offset by the higher nonresponse rates in those groups holding large amounts of liquid assets early in 1960. As a result the panels show successively smaller proportions of those with low liquid assets. In the 1960 sample 24.1 per cent of the spending units had no liquid assets whereas this group constituted only 19.3 per cent of the three-year panel. The effect noted with respect to liquid assets is equally pronounced with income (Table B-10). The moving population is disproportionately comprised of those with incomes under $5000 whereas the noninterview population is heavily weighted with those with incomes of $5000 or more. This is true in both years. The moving "effect" on the panel is stronger than the noninterview effect chiefly because the losses from moving are greater than the losses from noninterview. The net effect is an increase in the proportion of higher income spending units in the panels.

Table B-11 shows that the moving population is disporportionately concentrated among renters who moved in recently, among "other primaries," and among both types of secondaries (related and un-related). People who owned their homes in 1960 constituted disproportionately small proportions of the movers during the subsequent two years. As a result homeowners, who constituted 55 per cent of the 1960 sample, constituted 68 per cent of the three-year panel; renters, who composed 33 per cent of the original sample, comprised but 23 per cent of the three-year panel.

Table B-12 presents similar data by belt of residence. No very clear pattern emerges. For example, movers from the suburban areas of the smaller SMSA's constituted a disproportionately small portion of all movers during the year 1960-61, but a disproportionately high proportion of the movers over the year 1961-62. Nevertheless, one or two facts stand out. Moving rates are higher than average in the outlying areas and lower than average in the adjacent areas. Noninterview rates are high in central cities of both the largest SMSA's and of the other smaller SMSA's. Losses from noninterviews are disproportionately low in the outlying areas. The net result of moving losses and of noninterviews is that the panels have proportionately fewer spending units residing in the central cities of both larger and smaller SMSA's and a higher proportion in the adjacent areas. The high moving rates in the outlying areas combined with the low nonresponse rates there leave the proportion living in outlying areas virtually unchanged over the course of the two-year period.

Panel losses varied to some extent with the occupations of spending unit heads. Table B-13 shows that the spending units least likely to move are headed by managers, officials, and self-employed businessmen, by farmers, and by retired spending unit heads. The highest mobility, on the other hand, occurs among laborers and service workers and the miscellaneous and unemployed groups. It is interesting to note that those very groups characterized by high mobility have higher response rates. The reverse situation does not uniformly hold, however.

Spending unit heads aged 18-24 and 25-34 constituted a disproportionately high fraction of the moving population (Table B-14). Spending unit heads in the age categories 45-54 and 55-64 make up a large proportion of the noninterview population. Hence the two sources of loss to the panel, moving and nonresponse, have their major effects at different points in the age distribution, and these two types of losses tend to offset one another. However, due to the size of the moving group as compared to the noninterview group, the effects due to moving on the panel are always greater. Consequently both the two-year and three-year panels have disproportionately fewer young spending units.

To summarize Table B-8 through B-14, it is evident that the panels have an upward financial bias—that is, panels losses tend to be concentrated in the lower socioeconomic groups, primarily because of their higher mobility rates. Panel studies in which movers are not followed also have a disproportionately high number of homeowners as compared to renters or those who neither own nor rent. This ties in with the greater stability of the higher socio economic groups. Panels also tend to have a disproportionately large number of older spending units.

A quick review of the "not selected" column of Tables B-8 through B-14 reveals that there is a concentration in the lower educational, lower asset, and lower income categories. In the "not selected" group there are disproportionately few spending units living in suburban areas, and disproportionately many living in adjacent and outlying areas. There are disproportionately few professionals, managers, and proprietors; disproportionately many operatives, laborers and service workers, and retired spending unit heads. In addition, there are disproportionately few spending unit heads aged 25-44 and relatively many 65 or over in the "not selected" group.

Table B-1

1961 AND 1962 RATES OF RESPONSE AND OF RESIDENTIAL STABILITY FOR UNITS ORIGINALLY INTERVIEWED IN 1960,
BY EDUCATION OF SPENDING UNIT HEAD

(In per cent)

Education of head	1961 response rate among units still there in 1961	1962 response rate among units still there in 1962				Spending units interviewed in 1960 who remained unchanged at the same address	
		Address not visited in 1961[a]	Address visited in 1961[b]		Total	1961	1962
			1961 interview obtained	1961 interview not obtained			
8 years or less	84.1	87.4 (111)[c]	85.4 (371)	29.0 (36)	79.8	80.2	67.6
Some high school (9-11 years)	82.0	77.6 (54)	87.8 (229)	28.6 (37)	74.8	74.0	68.8
Completed high school	84.5	82.7 (52)	86.8 (302)	30.0 (33)	78.4	74.5	63.5
Some college	80.2	89.5 (19)	84.9 (139)	19.4 (19)	74.2	77.8	65.1
College degree	84.4	# (0)	88.7 (177)	38.2 (19)	80.6	75.3	65.5
Total[d]	83.3	84.4	86.5	28.8	77.8	76.4	66.2
Number of SU's still there[d]	1730	238	1224	145	1607		
Number of interviews obtained[d]	1434	201	1059	45	1303		

#Insufficient number of cases.

[a] The group whose addresses were not visited in 1961 is composed entirely of noncriterion addresses, i.e., they are the one-third of the noncriterion group not selected in 1961.

[b] The group whose addresses were visited in 1961 is composed of all criterion addresses plus two-thirds of the noncriterion addresses. The 1962 response rates have not been weighted to adjust for possible differences between these two groups.

[c] Figures in parentheses show the actual number of cases.

[d] Includes a few cases for which education was not ascertained.

Table B-2

1961 AND 1962 RATES OF RESPONSE AND OF RESIDENTIAL STABILITY FOR UNITS ORIGINALLY INTERVIEWED IN 1960, BY LIQUID ASSETS

(In per cent)

Liquid assets of spending unit (early in 1961)	1961 response rate among units still there in 1961	1962 response rate among units still there in 1962				Spending units interviewed in 1960 who remained unchanged at the same address	
		Address not visited in 1961[a]	Address visited in 1961[b]		Total	1961	1962
			1961 interview obtained	1961 interview not obtained			
None	83.7	82.4 (85)[c]	89.4 (199)	29.2 (27)	79.4	66.8	55.3
$1-499	88.7	86.8 (68)	87.9 (330)	19.1 (25)	81.0	73.8	62.3
$500-1999	83.5	87.8 (49)	84.5 (328)	27.6 (41)	76.1	79.2	73.0
$2000 or over	77.7	80.3 (36)	85.6 (367)	34.0 (52)	75.2	85.8	75.0
Total	83.3	84.4	86.5	28.8	77.8	76.4	66.2
Number of SU's still there	1730	238	1224	145	1607		
Number of interviews obtained	1434	201	1059	45	1305		

[a] The group whose addresses were not visited in 1961 is composed entirely of noncriterion addresses, i.e., they are the one-third of the noncriterion group not selected in 1961.

[b] The group whose addresses were visited in 1961 is composed of all criterion addresses plus two-thirds of the noncriterion addresses. The 1962 response rates have not been weighted to adjust for possible differences between these two groups.

[c] The numbers in parentheses show the actual number of cases.

Table B-3

1961 AND 1962 RATES OF RESPONSE AND OF RESIDENTIAL STABILITY FOR UNITS ORIGINALLY INTERVIEWED IN 1960,
BY INCOME

(In per cent)

Spending unit income in 1959	1961 response rate among units still there in 1961	1962 response rate among units still there in 1962				Spending units interviewed in 1960 who remained unchanged at the same address	
		Address not visited in 1961a	Address visited in 1961b			1961	1962
			1961 interview obtained	1961 interview not obtained	Total		
Under $3000	85.7	88.8 (98)c	85.5 (289)	27.3 (31)	80.2	71.9	61.3
$3000-4999	86.8	77.6 (58)	90.7 (236)	35.6 (25)	80.8	68.8	60.4
$5000-7499	82.7	84.0 (81)	87.1 (311)	21.0 (42)	76.2	80.9	70.0
$7500-9999	77.2	# (0)	87.8 (188)	36.8 (20)	79.2	84.0	72.2
$10,000 or over	80.1	# (1)	81.0 (200)	30.8 (27)	70.8	84.9	74.9
Total	83.3	84.4	86.5	28.8	77.8	76.4	66.2
Number of SU's still there	1730	238	1224	145	1607		
Number of interviews obtained	1434	201	1059	45	1305		

#Insufficient number of cases.

aThe group whose addresses were not visited in 1961 is composed entirely of noncriterion addresses, i.e., they are the one-third of the noncriterion group not selected in 1961.

bThe group whose addresses were visited in 1961 is composed of all criterion addresses plus two-thirds of the noncriterion addresses. The 1962 response rates have not been weighted to adjust for possible differences between these two groups.

cNumbers in parentheses show the actual number of cases.

Table B-4

1961 AND 1962 RATES OF RESPONSE AND OF RESIDENTIAL STABILITY FOR UNITS ORIGINALLY INTERVIEWED IN 1960, BY HOUSING STATUS AND DURATION

(In per cent)

Housing status and duration, early in 1960	1961 response rate among units still there in 1961	1962 response rate among units still there in 1962				Spending units interviewed in 1960 who remained unchanged at the same address	
		Address not visited in 1961a	Address visited in 1961b		Total	1961	1962
			1961 interview obtained	1961 interview not obtained			
Owners							
Purchased 1957-60	83.5	78.0 (41)c	88.1 (210)	35.1 (29)	77.0	87.6	83.5
Purchased before 1957	82.4	85.1 (121)	85.5 (657)	26.8 (65)	77.9	90.1	82.6
Renters							
Moved in 1957-60	87.4	80.8 (26)	88.9 (126)	# (9)	83.7	50.1	31.6
Moved in before 1957	81.7	86.2 (29)	86.3 (131)	13.9 (19)	74.1	82.0	65.3
Other primaries; unrelated	89.4	91.4 (12)	89.4 (47)	# (4)	85.3	59.0	48.3
Related secondaries	79.6	# (9)	84.9 (53)	28.6 (19)	70.8	60.2	50.3
Total	83.3	84.4	86.5	28.8	77.8	76.4	66.2
Number of SU's still there	1730	238	1224	145	1607		
Number of interviews obtained	1434	201	1059	45	1305		

#Insufficient number of cases.

aThe group whose addresses were not visited in 1961 is composed entirely of noncriterion addresses; i.e., they are the one-third of the noncriterion group not selected in 1961.

bThe group whose addresses were visited in 1961 is composed of all criterion addresses plus two-thirds of the noncriterion addresses. The 1962 response rates have not been weighted to adjust for possible differences between these two groups.

cNumbers in parentheses show the actual number of cases.

Table B-5

1961 AND 1962 RATES OF RESPONSE AND OF RESIDENTIAL STABILITY FOR UNITS ORIGINALLY INTERVIEWED IN 1960,
BY THE "BELT" CLASSIFICATION OF RESIDENCE

(In per cent)

Belt code (based on the 1950 Census)	1961 response rate among units still there in 1961	1962 response rate among units still there in 1962				Spending units interviewed in 1960 who remained unchanged at the same address	
		Address not visited in 1961[a]	Address visited in 1961[b]			1961	1962
			1961 interview obtained	1961 interview not obtained	Total		
Central cities of 12 largest SMSA's	77.5	75.9 (29)[c]	83.1 (154)	35.3 (28)	72.1	76.0	62.0
Central cities of other SMSA's	81.3	90.8 (33)	85.2 (176)	14.6 (21)	75.7	71.3	61.0
Suburban areas of 12 largest SMSA's	81.3	88.0 (25)	88.5 (191)	25.0 (25)	78.3	79.6	70.1
Suburban areas of other SMSA's	81.3	80.6 (31)	86.6 (164)	29.4 (17)	77.6	80.5	68.6
Adjacent areas	85.1	88.9 (54)	85.4 (254)	28.3 (27)	78.6	79.8	71.4
Outlying areas	89.2	81.8 (66)	88.8 (285)	37.5 (27)	81.5	73.0	64.4
Total	83.3	84.4	86.5	28.8	77.8	76.4	66.2
Number of SU's still there	1730	238	1224	145	1607		
Number of interviews obtained	1434	201	1059	45	1305		

[a] The group whose addresses were not visited in 1961 is composed entirely of noncriterion addresses, i.e., they are the one-third of the noncriterion group not selected in 1961.

[b] The group whose addresses were visited in 1961 is composed of all criterion addresses plus two-thirds of the noncriterion addresses. The 1962 response rates have not been weighted to adjust for possible differences between these two groups.

[c] The numbers in parentheses show the actual number of cases.

Table B-6

1961 AND 1962 RATES OF RESPONSE AND OF RESIDENTIAL STABILITY FOR UNITS ORIGINALLY INTERVIEWED IN 1960,
BY OCCUPATION OF SPENDING UNIT HEAD

(In per cent)

Occupation[a] of spending unit head, early 1960	1961 response rate among units still there in 1961	1962 response rate among units still there in 1962				Spending units interviewed in 1960 who remained unchanged at the same address	
		Address not visited in 1961[a]	Address visited in 1961[b]		Total	1961	1962
			1961 interview obtained	1961 interview not obtained			
White collar[c]	80.9	82.0 (50)[d]	85.7 (468)	30.2 (58)	76.3	77.8	68.0
Blue collar[c]	84.7	85.3 (109)	85.8 (466)	28.6 (56)	77.7	73.1	62.3
Farmer	86.3	88.2 (17)	92.3 (65)	# (9)	79.8	85.5	80.0
Unemployed	88.5	88.2 (17)	90.5 (63)	# (2)	90.1	71.8	61.0
Retired	82.4	82.2 (45)	87.0 (162)	25.0 (20)	76.8	81.8	71.0
Total	83.3	84.4	86.5	28.8	77.8	76.4	66.2
Number of SU's still there	1730	238	1224	145	1607		
Number of interviews obtained	1434	201	1059	45	1305		

#Insufficient number of cases.

[a]The group whose addresses were not visited in 1961 is composed entirely of noncriterion addresses, i.e., they are the one-third of the noncriterion group not selected in 1961.

[b]The group whose addresses were visited in 1961 is composed of all criterion addresses plus two-thirds of the noncriterion addresses. The 1962 response rates have not been weighted to adjust for possible differences between these two groups.

[c]"White collar" combines professional and technical workers, self-employed businessmen, managers and officials, and sales workers, and clerical workers. "Blue collar" combines craftsmen, foremen, operatives and kindred workers, laborers and service workers, and miscellaneous groups.

[d]Numbers in parentheses show the actual number of cases.

Table B-7

1961 AND 1962 RATES OF RESPONSE AND OF RESIDENTIAL STABILITY FOR UNITS ORIGINALLY INTERVIEWED IN 1960, BY AGE

(In per cent)

Age of SU head, early 1960	1961 response rate among units still there in 1961	1962 response rate among units still there in 1962				Spending units interviewed in 1960 who remained unchanged at the same address	
		Address not visited in 1961[a]	Address visited in 1961[b]		Total	1961	1962
			1961 interview obtained	1961 interview not obtained			
18-24	91.2	85.7 (7)[c]	88.9 (36)	66.7 (9)	83.8	45.4	29.1
25-34	85.3	86.4 (44)	89.9 (217)	23.4 (25)	79.8	66.0	55.5
35-44	84.5	84.8 (53)	85.6 (306)	28.4 (35)	77.1	78.9	72.5
45-54	79.5	81.8 (55)	85.2 (284)	31.3 (33)	76.6	84.1	74.6
55-64	81.6	90.3 (31)	86.2 (195)	16.2 (20)	77.8	88.1	71.6
65 and older	84.3	80.9 (47)	86.3 (182)	31.8 (23)	77.0	81.4	73.8
Total[d]	83.3	84.4	86.5	28.8	77.8	76.4	66.2
Number of SU's still there[d]	1730	238	1224	145	1607		
Number of interviews obtained[d]	1434	201	1059	45	1305		

[a] The group whose addresses were not visited in 1961 is composed entirely of noncriterion addresses, i.e., they are the one-third of the noncriterion group not selected in 1961.

[b] The group whose addresses were visited in 1961 is composed of all criterion addresses plus two-thirds of the noncriterion addresses. The 1962 response rates have not been weighted to adjust for possible differences between these two groups.

[c] The numbers in parentheses show the actual number of cases.

[d] Includes a few cases for which age of head was not ascertained.

Table B-8

DISTRIBUTION OF SPENDING UNIT HEADS BY AMOUNT OF EDUCATION AS OF EARLY 1960, TABULATED BY DISPOSITION IN PANEL IN ENSUING YEARS

(In per cent)

Education of SU head[a] (in early 1960)	1960 sample	Losses to 1960-61 panel			1960-61 panel	Losses to 1960-61 panel		1960-61-62 panel
		Not selected	Movers	Non-interviews		Movers	Non-interviews	
Eight years or less	32.3	43.7	26.9	31.7	33.4	34.7	36.1	32.7
9-11 years	19.2	20.2	22.0	20.7	18.7	16.1	17.8	19.4
12 years	25.7	26.7	28.1	23.2	25.3	26.7	24.3	25.2
Some college	11.4	9.3	11.0	13.9	11.3	12.0	11.9	11.0
College degree	11.4	0.1	12.0	10.5	11.3	10.5	9.9	11.7
Total	100.0	100.0	100.0	100.0	100.0	100.0	100.0	100.0
Number of cases	2887	642	515	296	1434	210	165	1059

[a]Spending unit heads for whom amount of education was not ascertained are assumed to be distributed proportionately with the rest of the population.

Table B-9

DISTRIBUTION OF SPENDING UNITS BY AMOUNT OF LIQUID ASSETS HOLDINGS EARLY IN 1960,
TABULATED BY DISPOSITION IN PANEL IN ENSUING YEARS

(In per cent)

Liquid assets (early 1960)	1960 sample	Not selected	Losses to 1960-61 panel		1960-61 panel	Losses to 1960-61-62 panel		1960-61-62 panel
			Movers	Non-interviews		Movers	Non-interviews	
None	24.1	34.9	33.6	20.4	21.0	33.8	14.9	19.3
$1-99	9.0	9.7	12.4	5.2	9.4	10.2	8.3	9.4
$100-199	6.6	7.5	7.2	4.2	6.6	6.9	5.4	6.7
$200-499	11.9	11.8	11.5	8.9	12.9	15.6	12.2	12.5
$500-999	12.3	10.9	12.3	9.0	12.8	7.4	18.9	13.0
$1000-1999	11.5	10.9	8.2	15.0	11.4	8.9	10.5	12.1
$2000-4999	13.4	10.4	7.7	18.9	14.1	8.7	18.6	14.6
$5000-9999	6.1	2.8	3.5	10.7	6.6	4.2	5.6	7.2
$10,000 or more	5.1	1.1	3.6	7.7	5.2	4.3	5.6	5.2
Total	100.0	100.0	100.0	100.0	100.0	100.0	100.0	100.0
Number of cases	2887	642	515	296	1434	210	165	1059
Median	$460	$170	$160	$1150	$500	$190	$740	$580

Table B-10

DISTRIBUTION OF SPENDING UNITS BY THEIR 1959 INCOME, TABULATED BY DISPOSITION OF PANEL IN ENSUING YEARS

(In per cent)

SU income in 1959	1960 sample	Losses to 1960-61 panel			1960-61 panel	Losses to 1960-61-62 panel		1960-61-62 panel
		Not selected	Movers	Non-interviews		Movers	Non-interviews	
Under $3000	28.9	40.5	33.7	23.0	27.4	33.2	27.9	26.2
$3000-4999	22.2	25.5	30.4	16.4	21.6	25.1	14.9	22.0
$5000-7499	26.2	33.2	21.0	28.6	27.3	25.4	27.4	27.6
$7500-9999	11.1	0.2	7.5	16.7	11.3	6.9	11.2	12.2
$10,000 or more	11.6	0.6	7.4	15.3	12.4	9.4	18.6	12.0
Total	100.0	100.0	100.0	100.0	100.0	100.0	100.0	100.0
Number of cases	2887	642	515	296	1434	210	165	1059

Table B-11

DISTRIBUTION OF SPENDING UNITS BY HOUSING STATUS AND DURATION IN EARLY 1960,
TABULATED BY DISPOSITION IN PANEL IN ENSUING YEARS

(In per cent)

Housing status and duration (early 1960)	1960 sample	Losses to 1960-61 panel			1960-61 panel	Losses to 1960-61-62 panel		1960-61-62 panel
		Not selected	Movers	Non-interviews		Movers	Non-interviews	
Owners								
Purchased in 1957-60	13.3	11.1	7.1	15.5	15.6	8.2	15.6	17.1
Purchased before 1957	41.9	40.9	17.0	50.6	47.4	21.0	56.0	51.4
Renters								
Moved 1957-60	21.1	22.3	46.0	10.8	15.0	37.0	9.0	11.4
Moved in before 1957	11.7	13.7	9.0	14.0	12.4	16.9	12.0	11.6
Other primaries; all unrelated secondaries	5.6	6.9	9.7	2.7	4.6	7.8	3.2	4.2
Related secondaries	6.4	5.1	11.2	6.4	5.0	9.1	4.2	4.3
Total	100.0	100.0	100.0	100.0	100.0	100.0	100.0	100.0
Number of cases	2887	642	515	296	1434	210	165	1059

Table B-12

DISTRIBUTION OF SPENDING UNITS BY "BELT" OF RESIDENCE IN 1960, TABULATED BY DISPOSITION IN PANEL IN ENSUING YEARS

(In per cent)

"Belt" of residence	1960 sample	Losses to 1960-61 panel			1960-61 panel	Losses to 1960-61-62 panel		1960-61-62 panel
		Not selected	Movers	Non-interviews		Movers	Non-interviews	
Central cities of 12 largest SMSA's	14.2	12.8	14.6	19.4	13.4	17.8	16.1	12.0
Central cities of other SMSA's	16.0	17.6	19.1	16.5	14.4	13.3	16.4	14.3
Suburban areas of 12 largest SMSA's	14.0	11.2	12.0	16.3	14.1	9.4	12.5	15.4
Suburban areas of other SMSA's	12.5	10.7	10.3	14.8	12.9	13.6	12.2	12.8
Adjacent areas	19.2	20.7	16.5	18.1	20.6	17.8	23.5	20.8
Outlying areas	24.1	27.0	27.5	14.9	24.6	28.1	19.3	24.7
Total	100.0	100.0	100.0	100.0	100.0	100.0	100.0	100.0
Number of cases	2887	642	515	296	1434	210	165	1059

Table B-13

DISTRIBUTION OF SPENDING UNITS BY OCCUPATION OF HEAD IN EARLY 1960,
TABULATED BY DISPOSITION IN PANEL IN ENSUING YEARS

(In per cent)

Occupation of head (early 1960)	1960 sample	Losses to 1960-61 panel			1960-61 panel	Losses to 1960-61-62 panel		1960-61-62 panel
		Not selected	Movers	Non-interviews		Movers	Non-interviews	
Professionals, technical workers	9.9	3.4	10.4	8.5	10.0	9.8	6.9	10.5
Managers, officials, etc.; self-employed businessmen	12.2	6.4	8.3	15.3	13.0	10.1	18.3	12.7
Clerical, sales workers	11.9	10.3	13.2	15.9	10.6	10.1	11.0	10.6
Craftsmen and foremen	12.4	11.7	12.5	13.9	12.9	11.6	16.6	12.6
Operatives	14.9	17.7	15.3	13.5	15.3	15.6	14.2	15.5
Laborers, service workers	11.4	17.0	13.9	8.5	10.3	14.0	9.5	9.7
Farmers, farm managers	4.6	5.5	2.7	4.1	5.2	4.4	3.2	5.6
Miscellaneous groups	3.7	4.7	6.6	1.4	2.8	4.4	2.0	2.7
Unemployed	5.5	6.5	6.8	3.7	5.7	6.0	4.4	5.8
Retired	13.5	16.8	10.3	15.2	14.2	14.0	13.9	14.3
Total	100.0	100.0	100.0	100.0	100.0	100.0	100.0	100.0
Number of cases	2887	642	515	296	1434	210	165	1059

Table B-14

DISTRIBUTION OF SPENDING UNITS BY AGE OF HEAD IN 1960,
TABULATED BY DISPOSITION IN PANEL IN ENSUING YEARS

(In per cent)

Age of SU head (early 1960)	1960 sample	Losses to 1960-61 panel			1960-61 panel	Losses to 1960-61-62 panel		1960-61-62 panel
		Not selected	Movers	Non-interviews		Movers	Non-interviews	
18-24	7.4	8.0	17.3	2.3	4.9	14.6	2.5	3.2
25-34	21.0	19.7	30.6	16.2	18.8	24.1	13.3	18.6
35-44	22.4	20.3	20.1	21.6	23.5	19.4	25.8	24.1
45-54	21.0	22.8	13.5	27.1	21.0	12.0	24.9	22.2
55-64	13.8	12.5	7.2	18.4	16.3	15.3	17.5	16.3
65 or older	14.4	16.7	11.3	14.4	15.5	14.6	16.0	15.6
Total	100.0	100.0	100.0	100.0	100.0	100.0	100.0	100.0
Number of cases	2887	642	515	296	1434	210	165	1059